Louis Becke

The Ebbing of the Tide

South Sea stories

Louis Becke

The Ebbing of the Tide
South Sea stories

ISBN/EAN: 9783744718134

Printed in Europe, USA, Canada, Australia, Japan

Cover: Foto ©Andreas Hilbeck / pixelio.de

More available books at **www.hansebooks.com**

THE EBBING OF THE TIDE

SOUTH SEA STORIES

BY

Louis Becke

AUTHOR OF "BY REEF AND PALM"

PHILADELPHIA
J. B. LIPPINCOTT COMPANY
1896

CONTENTS

	PAGE
"LULIBAN OF THE POOL"	1
NINIA	13
BALDWIN'S LOISÉ	37
AT A KAVA-DRINKING	63
MRS. LIARDET: A SOUTH SEA TRADING EPISODE	83
KENNEDY THE BOATSTEERER	91
A DEAD LOSS	101
HICKSON: A HALF-CASTE	113
A BOATING PARTY OF TWO	127
"THE BEST ASSET IN A FOOL'S ESTATE"	145
DESCHARD OF ONEAKA	157
NELL OF MULLINER'S CAMP	183
AURIKI REEF	199
AT THE EBBING OF THE TIDE	209
THE FALLACIES OF HILLIARD	217
A TALE OF A MASK	227
THE COOK OF THE "SPREETOO SANTOO"	237
LUPTON'S GUEST: A MEMORY OF THE EASTERN PACIFIC	245
IN NOUMÉA	265
THE FEAST AT PENTECOST	273
AN HONOUR TO THE SERVICE	281

"*LULIBAN OF THE POOL*"

"*Luliban of the Pool.*"

A BOY and a girl sat by the rocky margin of a deep mountain pool in Ponape in the North Pacific. The girl was weaving a basket from the leaves of a cocoanut. As she wove she sang the "Song of Luliban," and the boy listened intently.

"'Tis a fine song that thou singest, Niya," said the boy, who came from Metalanien and was a stranger; "and who was Luliban, and Red-Hair the White Man?"

"*O Guk!*" said Niya, wonderingly, "hast never heard in Metalanien of Luliban, she who dived with one husband and came up with another—in this very pool?"

"What new lie is this thou tellest to the boy because he is a stranger?" said a White Man, who lay resting in the thick grass waiting for the basket to be finished, for the three were going further up the mountain stream to catch crayfish.

"Lie?" said the child; "nay, 'tis no lie. Is not this the Pool of Luliban, and do not we sing the 'Song of Luliban,' and was not Red-Hair the White Man— he that lived in Jakoits and built the big sailing boat for Nanakin, the father of Nanakin, my father, the chief of Jakoits?"

"True, Niya, true," said the White Man, "I did but jest; but tell thou the tale to Sru, so that he may carry it home with him to Metalanien."

. . .

Then Niya, daughter of Nanakin, told Sru, the boy from Metalanien, the tale of Luliban of the Pool, and her husband the White Man called "Red-Hair," and her lover, the tattooed beachcomber, called "Harry from Yap."

. . .

"It was in the days before the fighting-ship went into Kiti Harbour and burnt the seven whaleships as they lay at anchor [1] that Red-Hair the White Man lived at Jakoits. He was a very strong man, and because that he was cunning and clever at fishing and killing the wild boar and carpentry, his house was full of riches, for Nanakin's heart was towards him always."

"Was it he who killed the three white men at Roăn Kiti?" asked the White Man.

"Aye," answered Niya, "he it was. They came in a little ship, and because of bitter words over the price of some tortoise-shell he and the men of Nanakin slew them. And Red-Hair burnt the ship and sank her. And for this was Nanakin's heart bigger than ever to Red-Hair, for out of the ship, before he burnt her, he took many riches—knives, guns and powder, and beads and pieces of silk; and half of all he gave to Nanakin."

"*Huh!*" said Sru, the boy. "He was a fine man!"

"Now, Harry from Yap and Red-Hair hated one

[1] The Shenandoah, in 1866.

another because of Luliban, whom Nanakin had given to Red-Hair for wife. This man, Harry, lived at Ngatik, the island off the coast, where the turtles breed, and whenever he came to Jakoits he would go to Red-Hair's house and drink grog with him so that they would both lie on the mats drunk together. Sometimes the name of Luliban would come between them, and then they would fight and try to kill each other, but Nanakin's men would always watch and part them in time. And all this was because that Luliban had loved Harry from Yap before she became wife to Red-Hair. The men favoured the husband of Luliban because of Nanakin's friendship to him, and the women liked best Harry from Yap because of his gay songs and his dances, which he had learnt from the people of Yap and Rŭk and Hogelu, in the far west; but most of all for his handsome figure and his tattooed skin.

"One day it came about that his grog was all gone, and his spirit was vexed, and Red-Hair beat Luliban, and she planned his death from that day. But Nanakin dissuaded her and said, 'It cannot be done; he is too great a man for me to kill. Be wise and forget his blows.'

"Then Luliban sent a messenger to Ngatik to Harry. He came and brought with him many square bottles of grog, and went in to Red-Hair's house, and they drank and quarrelled as they ever did; but because of what lay in his mind Harry got not drunk, for his eyes were always fixed on the face of Luliban.

"At last, when Red-Hair was fallen down on the mats, Luliban whispered to Harry, and he rose and lay down on a couch that was placed against the cane sides of the house. When all were asleep, Luliban stole outside and placed her face against the side of the house and called to Harry, who feigned to sleep. And then he and she talked for a long time. Then the white man got up and went to Nanakin, the chief, and talked long with him also.

"Said Nanakin the chief, 'O White Man, thou art full of cunning, and my heart is with thee. Yet what will it profit me if Red-Hair dies?'

"'All that is now his shall be thine,' said Harry.

"'And what shall I give thee?' said Nanakin.

"'Only Luliban,' said the White Man with the tattooed body.

. . . . .

"On the morrow, as the day touched the night, the people of Jakoits danced in front of Nanakin's house, and Harry, with flowers in his hair and his body oiled and stained with turmeric, danced also. Now among those who watched him was Luliban, and presently her husband sought her and drove her away, saying : 'Get thee to my house, little beast. What dost thou here watching this fool dance!'

"Harry but laughed and danced the more, and then Red-Hair gave him foul words. When the dance was ended, Harry went up to Red-Hair and said, 'Get thee home also, thou cutter of sleeping men's throats. I am a better man than thee. There is nothing that thou hast done that I cannot do.'

"Then Nanakin, whose mouth was ready with words put therein by Luliban, said, 'Nay, Harry, thou dost but boast. Thou canst not walk under the water in the Deep Pool with a heavy stone on thy shoulder—as Red-Hair has done.'

"'Bah!' said Harry. 'What he can do, that I can do.'

"Now, for a man to go in at one end of this pool here"—and Niya nodded her head to the waters at her feet—"and walk along the bottom and come out at the farther end is no great task, and as for carrying a heavy stone, that doth but make the task easier; but in those days there were devils who lived in a cave that is beneath where we now sit, and none of our people ever bathed here, for fear they would be seized and dragged down. But yet had Red-Hair one day put a stone upon his shoulder, and carried it under the water from one end of the pool to another—this to show the people that he feared no devils. But of the cave that can be gained by diving under the wall of rock he knew nothing—only to a few was it known.

"'Show this boaster his folly,' said Nanakin to Red-Hair, who was chewing his beard with wrath. And so it was agreed upon the morrow that the two white men should walk each with a stone upon his shoulder, in at one end of the deep pool and come out of the other, and Harry should prove his boast, that in all things he was equal to Red-Hair.

.   .   .   .   .

"When Red-Hair went back to his house Luliban was gone, and some said she had fled to the mountains, and he reproached Nanakin, saying: 'Thy daughter hath fled to Ngatik to the house of Harry. I will have her life and his for this.' But Nanakin smoothed his face and said: 'Nay, not so; but first put this boaster to shame before the people, and he shall die, and Luliban be found.'

"Now, Luliban was hid in another village, and

when the time drew near for the trial at the pool she went there before the people. In her hand she carried a sharp *toki* (tomahawk) and a long piece of strong cinnet with a looped end. She dived in and clambered out again underneath and waited. The cave is not dark, for there are many fissures in the top through which light comes when the sun is high.

"The people gathered round, and laughed and talked as the two white men stripped naked, save for narrow girdles of leaves round their loins. The skin of Red-Hair was as white as sand that lies always in the sun; that of Harry was brown, and covered from his neck to his feet with strange tattooing, more beautiful than that of the men of Ponape.

"They looked at each other with blood in their eyes, and the long, yellow teeth of Red-Hair ground together, but no words passed between them till Red-Hair, poising a great stone on his shoulder, called out to Harry: 'Follow me, O boastful stealer of my wife, and drown thy blue carcass.'

"Then he walked in, and Harry, also with a heavy stone, followed him. Ere one could count a score those that watched could not see Harry, because of the depth of the water and the darkness of his skin. But the white skin of Red-Hair gleamed like the belly of a shark when it turneth—then it disappeared.

"When they were half-way through a stone fell through a fissure of the cave, and Luliban, who watched for the signal, dived outwards with the line of cinnet, and came behind Red-Hair and put the noose over his left foot, and Harry, who followed close, cast the stone he carried away and raised his hand and stabbed him in the belly as he turned, and then, with

Luliban and he dragging tight the line of cinnet, they shot up from beneath the water into the cave and pulled Red-Hair after them.

. . . . .

"The people had gathered at the farther end of the pool to see the two men come up; and when they came not they wondered, and some one said: 'The devils have seized them!'

"Then Nanakin, who alone remained on the top of the rocks, called out, 'Alas for the white men! I can see bubbles, and the water is bloody,' and he beat his head on the rocks and made great grief and called out to the devils in the cave, 'Spare me my white men, O devils of the cave, spare me my good white men. But if one must die let it be him that hath offended.'

"Ah! he was a cunning man, was Nanakin, the father of Nanakin my father.

"The men and the women and children ran up again from the end of the pool; for, although they were greatly afraid, they durst not leave their chief by himself to beat out his head upon the stones. So they clustered round him and wailed also with him. And Nanakin raised his voice again and again and called out to the devils of the pool to spare him one white man; and the people called out with him. Yet none of them dared look upon the water of the pool; only Nanakin turned his eyes that way.

"At last the chief said, 'Ho, what is that?' and he pointed to the water, and they saw bubbles again rise up and break the surface of the water. 'Now shall I know if my white men are dead.'

"And, as they looked, behold there shot up from

the water a yellow gourd, and the men shouted, some in wonder and more in fear. And Nanakin leaned over the edge of the rock and stretched out his hand and drew the gourd to him. Then he took it in his hand, and lo! there was tied to the neck a piece of plaited cinnet, which ran deep down into the water under the rock.

"Again Nanakin called out to his men who stood crouched up behind him. 'What shall I do with this? shall I pull it up?'"

"And then—so the people said—there came a voice from the bowels of the earth, which said, 'Pull!'

"So they drew in the line, and as they drew it became heavy, and then something came up with a splash, and those that held the line looked over, and lo! there was the head of Red-Hair, wet and bloody, tied to the end of it by the ear.

"The head was laid upon the rock, and then the people would have turned and fled, but that Nanakin and two of his priests said there was now no fear as the cave devils were angry alone with Red-Hair, who had twice braved them.

"Then the two priests and Nanakin leant over the wall of rocks and called out again for the life of Harry to be spared, and as they called, he shot out from underneath and held out his hands; and they pulled him in.

"'Let us away from here quickly,' was all he said. 'I thank thee, O chief, for thy prayers; else had the devils of the pool taken off my head as they have taken off that of Red-Hair, and devoured my body as they have devoured his.'

"Then the people picked him up, for he was weak, and every one that was there left the pool in fear and trembling, except Nanakin and the two priests, who laughed inwardly.

"When all was quiet, Luliban, too, came up from under the water and dried her body, and oiled and scented her hair from a flask that she had hidden in the bushes, and went back to Red-Hair's house, and, with downcast face but a merry heart, asked her women to plead with her husband not to beat her for running away. Then they told her of the doings at the pool.

"When ten days were gone by for mourning, Luliban became wife to 'Harry from Yap,' and he took her with him to Ngatik, and the favour of Nanakin that was once Red-Hair's became his, and he prospered. And for long, long years no one knew how it was that Red-Hair lost his head till Luliban told it."

. . . . .

"*Huh!*" said Sru, the boy, admiringly. "He was a Fine Man, that Red-Hair; but the white man with the tattooed skin was a Better."

NINJA

Ninia.

AWAY out upon the wide Northern Pacific there is a group of three little islands. They are so very, very small that you need not seek to discover them on the map of the Pacific Ocean ; but if any of you have a chart of the North or West Pacific, then you would easily be able to find them. Run your eye up north, away past the Equator, in the direction of China, and you will see, to the north of New Guinea, a large cluster of islands named the "Caroline Islands," some of which are named, but most are not—only tiny dots no bigger than a pin's head serve to mark their position. Perhaps, however—if you get a German chart— you may see one of the largest of the small dots marked "Pingelap," and Pingelap is the name of the largest of the three little islands of my story ; the others are called Tugulu and Takai.

Now, although Pingelap and Tugulu and Takai are so close together that at low tide one may walk across the coral reef that encircles the whole group from one island to another, yet are they lonely spots, for there is no other island nearer than Mokil, which is ninety miles away.

But yet, although the three islands are so small, a great number of natives live upon them—between four and five hundred. There is only one village, which is on

Pingelap, and here all the people lived. The island itself is not more than two miles in length, and in no place is it more than a quarter of a mile in width; and Tugulu and Takai are still smaller. And from one end to the other the islands are covered with a dense verdure of cocoanut palms, with scarcely any other tree amongst them, so that when seen from the ship two or three miles away, they look exactly like a belt of emerald surrounding a lake of silver, for in their centre is a beautiful lagoon surrounded on three sides by the land, and on the west protected from the sweeping ocean rollers by a double line of coral reef stretching from little Takai to the south end of Pingelap.

There are hundreds of beautiful islands in the Pacific, but not any one of them can excel in beauty lonely little Pingelap. There are two reefs—an outer and an inner. Against the outer or ocean reef huge seas for ever dash unceasingly on the windward side of the island, and sometimes, in bad weather, will sweep right over the coral and pour through the shallow channel between Tugulu and Pingelap; and then the calm, placid waters of the lagoon will be fretted and disturbed until fine weather comes again. But bad weather is a rare event in those seas, and usually the lagoon of Pingelap is as smooth as a sheet of glass. And all day long you may see children paddling about in canoes, crossing from one shining beach to another, and singing as they paddle, for they are a merry-hearted race, the people of these three islands, and love to sing and dance, and sit out in front of their houses on moonlight nights and listen to tales told by the old men of the days when their islands were reddened with blood. For until fifteen years before, the people of Pingelap and Tugulu were at bitter enmity, and fought with and slaughtered each other to their heart's delight. And perhaps there would have soon been none left to tell the tale, but that one day an American whaleship, called the *Cohasset*, touched there to buy turtle from Sralik, the chief of Pingelap, and Sralik besought the captain to give him muskets and powder and ball to fight the Tugulans with.

So the captain gave him five muskets and plenty of powder and bullets, and then said—

"See, Sralik; I will give you a white man too, to show you how to shoot your enemies."

And then he laughed, and calling out to a man named Harry, he told him to clear out of the ship and go and live ashore and be a king, as he was not worth his salt as a boatsteerer.

And so this Harry Devine, who was a drunken, good-for-nothing, quarrelsome young American, came ashore with Sralik, and next day he loaded the five muskets and, with Sralik, led the Pingelap people over to Tugulu. There was a great fight, and as fast as Sralik loaded a musket, Harry fired it and killed a man. At last, when nearly thirty had been shot, the Tugulu people called for quarter.

"Get thee together on Takai," called out Sralik, "and then will we talk of peace."

Now Takai is such a tiny little spot, that Sralik knew he would have them at his mercy, for not one of them had a musket.

As soon as the last of the Tugulu people had crossed the shallow channel that divides Tugulu from Takai, the cunning Sralik with his warriors lined the beach and then called to the Tugulans—

"This land is too small for so many."

And then Harry, once the boatsteerer and now the beachcomber, fired his muskets into the thick, surging mass of humanity on the little islet, and every shot told. Many of them, throwing aside their spears and clubs, sprang into the water and tried to swim over to Pingelap across the lagoon. But Sralik's men pursued them in canoes and clubbed and speared them as they swam; and some that escaped death by club or spear, were rent in pieces by the sharks which, as soon as they smelt the blood of the dead and dying men that sank in the quiet waters of the lagoon, swarmed in through a passage in the western reef. By and by the last of those who took to the water were killed, and only some eighty or ninety men and many more women and children were left on Takai, and the five muskets became so hot and foul that Harry could murder no longer, and his arm was tired out with slaughter.

All that night Sralik's warriors watched to see that none escaped, and at dawn the hideous massacre began again, and club, spear, and musket did their fell work till only the women and children were left. These were spared. Among them was Ninia, the wife of Sikra, the chief of Tugulu. And because she was young and fairer than any of the others, the white man asked her of Sralik for his wife. Sralik laughed.

"Take her, O clever white man—her and as many more as thou carest for slaves. Only thou and I shall rule here now in this my island."

So Harry took her and married her according to native custom, and Ninia was his one wife for nearly fifteen years, when one day he was quietly murdered as he lay asleep in his house with his wife and two children; and although Sralik wept loudly and cut his great chest with a shark's teeth dagger, and offered sacrifices of turtle flesh to the white man's *jelin*, Ninia his wife and many other people knew that it was by Sralik's orders that Harry had been killed, for they had quarrelled over the possession of a whaleboat which Harry had bought from a passing ship, and which he refused to either sell or give to Sralik.

However, Sralik was not unkind to Ninia, and gave her much of her dead husband's property, and told her that he would give her for an inheritance for her two daughters the little islet—Takai.

And there in the year 1870 Ninia the widow, and Ninia her eldest daughter (for on Pingelap names of the first-born are hereditary) and Tarita, the youngest, went to live. With them went another girl, a granddaughter of the savage old Sralik. Her name was Ruvani. She was about eleven years of age, and as pretty as a gazelle, and because of her great friendship for Ninia—who was two years older than she—she had wept when she saw the mother and daughters set out for Takai.

Fierce-hearted Sralik coming to the doorway of his thatched hut heard the sound of weeping, and looking out he saw Ruvani sitting under the shade of some banana trees with her face hidden in her pretty brown hands.

When he learned the cause of her grief his heart softened, and drawing his little grand-daughter to him, patted her head, and said—

"Nay, weep not, little bird. Thou too shalt go to Takai; and see, because of thee my heart shall open wide to Ninia and her daughters, and I will give her four slaves—two men and two women—who shall toil for you all. And when thou art tired of living at Takai, then thou and thy two playmates shall come over here to me and fill my house with the light of thy eyes.

So that is how Ninia, the widow of the wandering white man, and her two daughters and their friend came to live at the little islet called Takai.

II.

The months went by and Ruvani, the chief's granddaughter, still lived with her friends, for she was too happy to leave them. Sometimes, though, on bright moonlight nights, the three girls would paddle across to the big village and gather with the rest of the village girls in front of the chief's house, and dance and sing and play the game called *n'jiajia;* and then, perhaps, instead of going home across the lagoon in the canoe, they would walk around on the inner beaches of Pingelap and Tugulu. And long ere they came to the house they could see the faint glimmer of the fire within, beside which Ninia the widow slept awaiting their return.

Stealing softly in, the girls would lie down together on a soft white mat embroidered with parrots' feathers that formed their bed, and pulling another and larger one over them for a coverlet, they would fall asleep, undisturbed by the loud, hoarse notes of a flock of *katafa* (frigate birds) that every night settled on the boughs of a great *koa* tree whose branches overhung the house.

Sometimes when the trade-winds had dropped, and the great ocean rollers would beat heavily upon the far-off shelves of the outer reef, the little island would seem to shake and quiver to its very foundations, and now and then as a huge wave would curl slowly over and break with a noise like a thunder-peal, the frigate-birds would awake from their sleep and utter a solemn answering squawk, and the three girls nestling closer together would whisper—

"'Tis Nanawit, the Cave-god, making another cave."

Ere the red sun shot out from the ocean the eight dwellers on Takai would rise from their mats; and whilst Ninia the widow would kindle a fire of broken cocoanut shells, the two men slaves would go out and bring back young cocoanuts and taro from the plantation on Tugulu, and their wives would take off their gaily-coloured grass-girdles and tie coarse *nairiris* of cocoanut fibre around them instead, and with the three girls go out to the deep pools on the reef and catch fish. Sometimes they would surprise a turtle in one of the pools, and, diving in after the frightened creature, would capture and bring it home in triumph to Ninia the widow.

Such was the daily life of those who dwelt on Takai.

.   .   .   .   .

One day, ere the dews of the night had vanished from the lofty plumes of the cocoanut palms, there came to them a loud cry, borne across the waters of the silent lagoon, over from the village—

"A ship! A ship!"

Now not many ships came to Pingelap—perhaps

now and then some wandering sperm-whaler, cruising lazily along toward the distant Pelew Islands, would heave-to and send a boat ashore to trade for turtle and young drinking cocoanuts. But it was long since any whaleship had called, and Ninia the widow, as she looked out seawards for the ship, said to the girls—

"'Tis not yet the season for the whaleships; four moons more and we may see one. I know not what other ships would come here."

By and by they saw the ship. She sailed slowly round the south point of Pingelap and backed her foreyard, and presently a boat was lowered and pulled ashore.

Little Tarita, clapping her hands with joy, darted into the house, followed by Ruvani and Ninia, and casting off their wet girdles of banana fibre—for they had just come in from fishing—they dressed themselves in their pretty *nairiris* of coloured grasses, and put on head-dresses of green and gold parrots' feathers, with necklaces of sweet-smelling berries around their necks, and were soon paddling across the lagoon to see the white strangers from the ship, who had already landed and gone up the beach and into the village.

It is nearly a mile from Takai to the village, and before the girls reached there they heard a great clamour of angry voices, and presently two white men dressed in white and carrying books in their hands came hurriedly down the beach, followed by a crowd of Sralik's warriors, who urged them along and forced them into the boat.

Then seizing the boat they shot her out into the water, and, shaking their spears and clubs, called out—

"Go, white men, go!"

Ninia.

But although the native sailors who pulled the boat were trembling with fear, the two white men did not seem frightened, and one of them, standing up in the stern of the boat, held up his hand and called out to the angry and excited people—

"Let me speak, I pray you!"

The natives understood him, for he spoke to them in the language spoken by the natives of Strong's Island, which is only a few hundred miles from Pingelap.

. . . . .

The people parted to the right and left as Sralik, the chief, with a loaded musket grasped in his brawny right hand, strode down to the water's edge. Suppressed wrath shone in his eyes as he grounded his musket on the sand and looked at the white man.

"Speak," he said, "and then be gone."

The white man spoke.

"Nay, spare us thy anger, O chief. I come not here to fill thy heart with anger, but with peace; and to tell thee of the great God, and of His Son Christ, who hath sent me to thee."

Sralik laughed scornfully.

"Thou liest. Long ago did I know that some day a white-painted ship would come to Pingelap, and that white men would come and speak to us of this new God and His Son who is called Christ, and would say that this Christ had sent them, and then would the hearts of my people be stolen from Nanawit the Cave-god, and Tuarangi the god of the Skies, and I, Sralik the king, would become but as a slave, for this new God of theirs would steal the hearts of my people from me as well."

The white man said sorrowfully—

"Nay, that is not so. Who hath told thee this?"

"A better white man than thee—he who slew my enemies and was named Haré (Harry). Long ago did he warn me of thy coming and bid me beware of thee with thy lies about thy new God and His Son Christ."

Again the missionary said—

"Let me speak."

But Sralik answered him fiercely—

"Away, I tell thee, to thy white-painted ship, and trouble me no more," and he slapped the stock of his musket, and his white teeth gleamed savagely through his bearded face.

So the two missionaries went back, and the *Morning Star* filled away again and sailed slowly away to the westward.

.   .   .   .   .

That night as the three girls lay on the mats beside the dying embers of the fire, they talked of the strange white men whom Sralik had driven away.

Ninia the widow listened to them from her corner of the house, and then she said musingly—

"I, too, have heard of this God Christ; for when Haré, thy father, lay in my arms with the blood pouring from his wound and death looked out from his eyes, he called upon His name."

Young Ninia and her sister drew closer and listened. Never until now had they heard their mother speak of their white father's death. They only knew that some unknown enemy had thrust a knife into his side as he lay asleep, and Ninia the widow had, with terror in her eyes, forbidden them to talk of it even amongst

Ninia.

themselves. Only she herself knew that Sralik had caused his death. But to-night she talked.

"Tell us more, my mother," said girl Ninia, going over to her, and putting her cheek against her mother's troubled face and caressing her in the darkness.

"Aye, I can tell thee now, my children, for Sralik's anger is dead now. . . . It was at the dawn, just when the first note of the blue pigeon is heard, that I heard a step in the house—'twas the death-men of Sralik—and then a loud cry, and Haré, thy father, awoke to die. The knife had bitten deep and he took my hands in his and groaned.

"'Farewell,' he said, 'O mother of my children, I die!' Then he cried, 'And Thou, O Christ, look down on and forgive me; Christ the Son of God.'

"With my hand pressed to his side, I said: 'Who is it that thou callest upon, my husband? Is it the white man's God?'

"'Aye,' he said, 'this Christ is He whom I have so long denied. He is the Son of the God whose anger I fear to meet now that my soul goes out into darkness.'

"'Fear not,' I said, weeping, 'I, Ninia, will make offerings to this white God and His Son Christ, so that their anger may be softened against thy spirit when it wanders in ghost-land.'

"So he groaned and was dead. And for six or more moons did I put offerings to the white God upon thy father's grave as I had promised. No offerings made I to our own gods, for he despised them even as he despised his own. But yet do I think his *jelin* (spirit) is at rest in ghost-land; else had it come to me in the night and touched me on the forehead as I slept."

III.

A month had gone by since the day that Sralik had driven away the "Christ ship," as the people called the *Morning Star*, and then word came over from Sralik to Ruvani, his granddaughter, to come over and take her part in a night-dance and feast to the rain-god, for the year had been a good one and the cocoanut trees were loaded with nuts. For this was the dancing and feasting.

All that day the eight people of Takai were busied in making ready their gifts of food for the feast which was to take place in two days' time. In the afternoon, when the sun had lost its strength, the three girls launched their canoe and set out for a place on the northern point of Pingelap, where grew in great profusion the sweet-smelling *nudu* flower. These would they get to make garlands and necklets to wear at the great dance, in which they were all to take part.

In an hour or two they had gathered all the *nudu* flowers they desired, and then little Tarita looking up saw that the sky was overcast and blackening, and presently some heavy drops of rain fell.

"Haste, haste," she cried to the others, "let us away ere the strong wind which is behind the black clouds overtakes us on the lagoon."

Night comes on quickly in the South Seas, and by the time they had seated themselves in the canoe it was dark. In a little while a sharp rain-squall swept down from the northward, and they heard the wind rattling and crashing through the branches of the palms on Tugulu.

Ninia, who was steering, boldly headed the canoe across the lagoon for Takai, and laughed when Ruvani and Tarita, who were wet and shivering with the cold rain, urged that they should put in at the beach on Tugulu and walk home.

"Paddle, paddle strongly," she cried, "what mattereth a little rain and wind! And sing, so that our mother will hear us and make ready something to eat. Look, I can already see the blaze of her fire."

Striking their paddles into the water in unison, they commenced to sing, but suddenly their voices died away in terror as a strange, droning hum was borne down to them from the black line of Tugulu shore; and then the droning deepened into a hoarse roaring noise as the wild storm of wind and fierce, stinging rain tore through the groves of cocoanuts and stripped them of leaves and branches.

Brave Ninia, leaning her lithe figure well over the side of the canoe, plunged her paddle deep down and tried to bring the canoe head to wind to meet the danger, and Ruvani, in the bow, with long hair flying straight out behind her, answered her effort with a cry of encouragement, and put forth all her strength to aid.

But almost ere the cry had left her lips, the full fury of the squall had struck them; the canoe was caught in its savage breath, twirled round and round, and then filled.

"Keep thou in the canoe, little one, and bale," cried Ninia to Tarita, as she and Ruvani leaped into the water.

For some minutes the two girls clung with one hand each to the gunwale, and Tarita, holding the large wooden *ahu*, or baler, in both hands, dashed the water out. Then she gave a trembling cry—the baler struck against the side of the canoe and dropped overboard.

Ninia dared not leave the canoe to seek for it in the intense darkness, and so clinging to the little craft, which soon filled again, they drifted about. The waters of the lagoon were now white with the breaking seas, and the wind blew with fierce, cruel, steadiness, and although they knew it not, they were being swept quickly away from the land towards the passage in the reef.

The rain had ceased now, and the water being warm none of them felt cold, but the noise of the wind and sea was so great that they had to shout loudly to each other to make their voices heard.

Presently Ruvani called out to Ninia—

"Let us take Tarita between us and swim to the shore, ere the sharks come to us."

"Nay, we are safer here, Ruvani. And how could we tell my mother that the canoe is lost? Let us wait a little and then the wind will die away."

Canoes are valuable property on Pingelap, where suitable wood for building them is scarce, and this was in Ninia's mind.

They still kept hold of their paddles, and although afraid of the sharks, waited patiently for the storm to cease, little thinking that at that moment the ebbing tide and wind together had swept them into the passage, and that they were quickly drifting away from their island home.

. . . . .

All that night Ninia the widow and her four slaves

sought along the beach of Tugulu for the three girls, who they felt sure had landed there. And when the day broke at last, and they saw that the gale had not ceased and that the canoe had vanished, they ran all the way over to the village, and Ninia threw herself at Sralik's feet.

"Thy granddaughter and my children have perished, O chief."

The chief came to the door of his house and looked out upon the wild turmoil of waters.

"It is the will of the gods," he said, "else had not my whaleboat been crushed in the night," and he pointed to the ruins of the boat-shed upon which a huge cocoanut tree had fallen and smashed the boat.

Then he went back into his house and covered his face, for Ruvani was dear to his savage old heart.

And Ninia went back to her lonely house and wept and mourned for her lost ones as only mothers weep and mourn, be they of white skins or brown.

. . . . .

Away out into the ocean the canoe was swept along, and Ruvani and Ninia still clung to her, one at the head and one at the stern. Once there came a brief lull, and then they succeeded in partly freeing her from water, and Tarita using her two hands like a scoop meanwhile, the canoe at last became light enough for them to get in.

They were only just in time, for even then the wind freshened, and Ninia and Ruvani let the canoe run before it, for they were too exhausted to keep her head to the wind.

When daylight broke Ninia, with fear in her heart, stood up in the canoe and looked all round her.

There was no land in sight! Poor children! Even then they could not have been more than twenty miles away from the island, for Pingelap is very low and not visible even from a ship's deck at more than twelve or fifteen miles.

But she was a brave girl, although only fourteen, and when Tarita and Ruvani wept she encouraged them.

"Sralik will come to seek us in the boat," she said, although she could have wept with them.

The wind still carried them along to the westward, and Ninia knew that every hour was taking them further and further away from Pingelap, but, although it was not now blowing hard, she knew that it was useless for them to attempt to paddle against it. So, keeping dead before the wind and sea, they drifted slowly along.

At noon the wind died away, and then, tired and worn out, she and Ruvani lay down in the bottom of the canoe and slept, while little Tarita sat up on the cane framework of the outrigger and watched the horizon for Sralik's boat.

Hour after hour passed, and the two girls still slept. Tarita, too, had lain her weary head down and slumbered with them.

Slowly the sun sank beneath a sea of glassy smoothness, unrippled even by the faintest air, and then Ninia awoke, and, sitting up, tossed her cloud of dark hair away from her face, and looked around her upon the darkening ocean. Her lips were dry and parched, and she felt a terrible thirst.

"Tarita," she called, "art sleeping, dear one?"

A sob answered her.

"Nay, for my head is burning, and I want a drink."

.   .   .   .

The whole story of those days of unutterable agony cannot be told here. There, under a torrid sun, without a drop of water or a morsel of food, the poor creatures drifted about till death mercifully came to two of them.

It was on the evening of the second day that Ninia, taking her little sister in her own fast weakening arms, pressed her to her bosom, and, looking into her eyes, felt her thirst-racken body quiver and then grow still in the strange peacefulness of death. Then a long wailing cry broke upon the silence of the night.

How long she had sat thus with the child's head upon her bosom and her dead sightless eyes turned upward to the glory of the star-lit heavens she knew not; after that one moaning cry of sorrow that escaped from her anguished heart she had sat there like a figure of stone, dull, dazed, and unconscious almost of the agonies of thirst. And then Ruvani, with wild, dreadful eyes and bleeding, sun-baked lips, crept towards her, and, laying her face on Ninia's hand, muttered—

"Farewell, O friend of my heart; I die."

And then, as she lay there with closed eyes and loosened hair falling like a shroud over the form of her dead playmate, she muttered and talked, and then laughed a strange weird laugh that chilled the blood in Ninia's veins. So that night passed, and then, as the fiery sun uprose again upon the wide sweep or lonely sea and the solitary drifting canoe with its load of misery, Ruvani, who still muttered and laughed to herself, suddenly rose up, and with the strength of madness, placing her arms around the stiffened form of little Tarita, she sprang over the side and sank with her.

Ninia, stretching her arms out piteously, bowed her head, and lay down to die.

.   .   .   .   .

She was aroused from her stupor by the cries of a vast flock of sea birds, and, opening her eyes, she saw that the canoe was surrounded by thousands upon thousands of bonita that leaped and sported and splashed about almost within arm's length of her. They were pursuing a shoal of small fish called *atuli*, and these every now and then darted under the canoe for protection. Sometimes, as the hungry bonita pressed them hard, they would leap out of the water, hundreds together, and then the sea birds would swoop down and seize them ere they fell back into the sea.

Ninia, trembling with excitement and the hope of life, watched eagerly. Presently she heard a curious, rippling noise, and then a rapidly-repeated tapping on the outrigger side of the canoe.

Oh! the joy of it; the water was black with a mass of *atuli*, crowded together on the surface, and frightened and exhausted.

She thrust her hands in among them and threw handsful after handsful into the canoe, and then her dreadful thirst and hunger made her cease, and, taking fish after fish, she bit into them with her sharp teeth, and assuaged both hunger and thirst.

As she tore ravenously at the *atuli* the sky became overcast, and while the bonitas splashed and jumped around her, and the birds cried shrilly overhead, the blessed rain began to fall, at first in heavy drops, and then in a steady downpour.

Taking off her thick grass girdle, she rolled it up into a tight coil and placed it across the bottom of the canoe, about two feet from the bows, so as to form a dam; and then, lying face downwards, she drank and drank till satisfied. Then she counted the *atuli*. There were over forty.

All that day the rain squalls continued, and then the wind settled and blew steadily from the east, and Ninia kept the canoe right before it.

That night she slept but little. A wild hope had sprung up in her heart that she might reach the island of Ponape, which she knew was not many days' sail from Pingelap. Indeed, she had once heard her father and Sralik talking about going there in the whaleboat to sell turtle-shell to the white traders there.

But she did not know that the current and trade wind were setting the canoe quickly away from Ponape towards a group of low-lying atolls called Ngatik.

. . . . .

The rain had ceased, and in the warm, starlight night she drifted on to the west, and as she drifted she dreamed of her father, and saw Ninia the widow, her mother, sitting in the desolate house on Takai, before the dying embers of the fire, and heard her voice crying :

"*O thou white Christ God, to whom my husband called as he died, tell me are my children perished? I pray thee because of the white blood that is in them to protect them and let me behold my beloved again.*"

The girl awoke. Her mother's voice seemed to still murmur in her ears, and a calm feeling of rest entered her soul. She took her paddle, and then stopped and thought.

This new God—the Christ-God of her father—perhaps He would help her to reach the land. She, too, would call upon Him, even as her mother had done.

"See, O Christ-God. I am but one left of three. I pray Thee guide my canoe to land, so that I may yet see Ninia my mother once more."

As the dawn approached she dozed again, and then she heard a sound that made her heart leap—it was the low, monotonous beat of the surf.

When the sun rose she saw before her a long line of low-lying islands, clothed in cocoanuts, and shining like jewels upon the deep ocean blue.

She ate some more of the fish, and, paddling as strongly as her strength would permit, she passed between the passage, entered the smooth waters of the lagoon, and ran the canoe up on to a white beach.

"The Christ-God has heard me," she said as she threw her wearied form under the shade of the cocoanut palms and fell into a heavy, dreamless slumber.

And here next morning the people of Ngatik found her. They took the poor wanderer back with them to their houses that were clustered under the palm-groves a mile or two away, and there for two years she dwelt with them, hoping and waiting to return to Pingelap.

One day a ship came—a whaler cruising back to Strong's Island and the Marshall Group. The captain was told her story by the people of Ngatik, and offered to touch at Pingelap and land her.

. . . . .

Ninia.

Ninia the widow was still living on Takai, and her once beautiful face had grown old and haggard-looking. Since the night of the storm four ships had called at Pingelap, but she had never once gone over to the village, for grief was eating her heart away; and so, when one evening she heard that a ship was in sight, she took no heed.

Her house was very sad and lonely now, and as night came on she lay down in her end of the house and slept, while the other four people sat round the fire and talked and smoked.

In the middle of the night the four slaves got up and went away to the village, for they wanted to be there when the boat from the ship came ashore.

At daylight the ship was close in, and the people in the village saw a boat lowered. Then a cry of astonishment burst from them when they saw the boat pull straight in over the reef and land at Takai, about a hundred yards from the house of Ninia, the white man's widow.

Only one person got out, and then the boat pushed off again and pulled back to the ship.

. . . . . .

Ninia the widow had risen, and was rolling up the mat she had slept upon, when a figure darkened the doorway. She turned wonderingly to see who it was that had come over so early from the village, when the stranger, who was a tall, graceful young girl, sprang forward, and, folding her arms around her, said, sobbing with joy—

"My mother. . . . The Christ-God hath brought me back to thee again."

BALDWIN'S LOISÉ

Baldwin's Loisé.

Miss Lambert.

Her mother was a full-blooded native—a woman of Anaa, in the Chain Islands—her father a dissolute and broken white wanderer. At the age of ten she was adopted by a wealthy South Sea trading captain, living on the East Coast of New Zealand. He, with his childless wife, educated, cared for, and finally loved her, as they once loved a child of their own, dead twenty years before.

At sixteen Loisé was a woman; and in the time that had passed since the morning she had seen her reckless, beach-combing father carried ashore at Nukutavake with a skinful of whisky and his pockets full of the dollars for which he had sold her, the tongue and memories of her mother's race had become, seemingly, utterly forgotten.

. . . . .

But only seemingly; for sometimes in the cold winter months, when savage southerly gales swept over the cloud-blackened ocean from the white fields of Antarctic ice and smote the New Zealand coast with chilling blast, the girl would crouch beside the fire in Mrs. Lambert's drawing-room, and covering herself with warm rugs, stare into the glowing coals until she fell asleep.

She had not forgotten.

One day a visitor came to see her adopted father. He was captain of a small trading schooner running to the Paumotus—her mother's land—and although old Lambert had long since given up his trading business and voyagings, he liked to meet people from the Islands, and, indeed, kept open house to them; so both he and Mrs. Lambert made him welcome.

The captain of the schooner was a man of a type common enough in the South Seas, rough, good-humoured, and coarsely handsome.

After dinner the two men sat over their whisky and talked and smoked. Mrs. Lambert, always an invalid, had gone to her room, but Loisé, book in hand, lay on a sofa and seemed to read. But she did not read, she listened. She had caught a word or two uttered by the dark-faced, black-bearded skipper—words that filled her with vague memories of long ago. And soon she heard names—names of men, white and brown, whom she had known in that distant, almost forgotten and savage childhood.

. . . . .

When the seaman rose to leave and extended his tanned, sinewy hand to the beautiful "Miss Lambert," and gazed with undisguised admiration into her face, he little thought that she longed to say, "Stay and let me hear more." But she was conventional enough to know better than that, and that her adopted parents would be genuinely shocked to see her anything more than distantly friendly with such a man as a common trading captain—even though that man had once been one of Lambert's most trusted men. Still, as she raised her eyes to his, she murmured softly, "We will be glad to see you again, Captain Lemaire." And the dark-faced seaman gave her a subtle, answering glance.

. . . . .

All that night she lay awake—awake to the child memories of the life that until now had slumbered within her. From her opened bedroom window she could see the dulled blaze of the city's lights, and hear ever and anon the hoarse and warning roar of a steamer's whistle. She raised herself and looked out upon the waters of the harbour. A huge, black mass was moving slowly seaward, showing only her mast-head and side-lights—some ocean tramp bound northward. Again the boom of the whistle sounded, and then, by the quickened thumping of the propeller, the girl knew that the tramp had rounded the point and was heading for the open sea.

. . . . .

She lay back again on the pillow and tried to sleep. Why couldn't she sleep, she wondered. She closed her eyes. The branches of the pine that grew close to her window rustled and shook to a passing breath of wind, and her eyes opened again. How strangely, though, it sounded to-night, and how her heart was thumping! Again the white lids drooped and half closed again, and the pine branches waved and soughed gently to the breeze.

And then the dead grey of the wall of the room changed to a bright, shimmering white—the white of an island beach as it changes, under the red flush of the morn, from the shadows of the night to a broad belt of gleaming silver—and the sough of the pine-tree by the window deepened into the humming music of the trade-wind when it passes through the sleeping palms, and a million branches awake trembling to its first breaths and shake off in pearly showers the dews of the night. Again she raced along the clinking sand with her childish, half-naked companions, and heard the ceaseless throb of the beating surf upon the windward reef, and saw the flash of gold and scarlet of a flock of parrakeets that with shrill, whistling note, vanished through the groves of cocoa-nuts as they sped mountainwards. Then her latent native soul awoke and made her desperate.

· · · · ·

Ere two days had passed she was missing, and six weeks later a little white-painted schooner hove-to off one of the Paumotu Group, lowered a boat, and landed her amongst the wondering natives.

The dark-faced, black-bearded man who steered the boat held her hand a moment ere he said good-bye.

"It is not too late, Loisé."

She raised her face and laughed scornfully.

"To go back? To go back to hear the old man who was a father and the good woman who was a mother to me, tell me that they hated and despised me!" And then quick, scalding tears.

The man's face flushed. "No, not that, but," with an oath, "look here, if you'll come with me I'll head the schooner for Tahiti, and as soon as she swings to her anchor we will be ashore and married."

She shook her head. "Let me go, Captain Lemaire.

Whatever comes to me, 'tis I alone who must answer for it. And so—good-bye."

. . . .

She stood and watched the boat hoisted to the davits, and saw the schooner slowly gather way, and then glide past and disappear round the palm-crowned point. Then she turned with streaming eyes and choking voice to the brown-skinned people that stood around her, and spoke to them in her mother's tongue.

So ended the sixteen years' life of the beautiful Miss Lambert and began that of Loisé, the half-blood.

Loisé, the Half-blood.

There was a wild rush of naked, scurrying feet, and a quick panting of brown bosoms along the winding path that led to Baldwin's house at Rikitea. A trading schooner had just dropped anchor inside the reef, and the runners, young lads and girls—half-naked, lithe-limbed and handsome—like all the people of the "thousand isles," wanted to welcome Baldwin the Trader at his own house door.

. . .

Two of them—a boy and girl—gained the trader's gate ahead of their excited companions, and, leaning their backs against the white palings, mocked the rest for their tardiness in the race. With one arm around the girl's lissom waist, the boy, Maturei, short, thickset, muscular, and the bully of the village, beat off with his left hand those who sought to displace them from the gate; and the girl, thin, creole-faced, with soft, red-lipped mouth, laughed softly at their vexation. Her gaily-coloured grass waist girdle had broken, and presently moving the boy's protecting arm, she tried to tie the band, and as she tied it she rattled out oaths in English and French at the score of brown hands that sought to prevent her.

"*Hui! Hui!!* Away, ye fools, and let me tie my girdle," she said in the native tongue. "'Tis no time now for such folly as this; for, see, the boat is lowered from the ship and in a little time the master will be here."

The merry chatter ceased in an instant and every face turned towards the schooner, and a hundred pair of curious eyes watched. Then, one by one, they sat down and waited; all but the two at the gate, who remained standing, the boy's arm still wound round the girl's waist.

* * * * *

The boat was pulling in swiftly now, and the "click-clack" of the rowlocks reached the listening ears of those on shore.

There were two figures in the stern, and presently one stood up, and taking off his hat, waved it towards the shore.

A roar of welcome from the thronging mass of natives that lined the beach drowned the shrill, piping treble of the children round the gate, and told sturdy old Tom Baldwin that he was recognised, and scarce had the bow of the boat ploughed into the soft sand of the beach when he was seized upon and smothered with caresses, the men with good-natured violence thrusting aside the women and forming a body-guard to conduct him and the young man with him from the boat to the house. And about the strange white man the people thronged with inquiring and admiring glances, for he was big and strong-looking—and that to a native mind is better than all else in the world.

With joyous, laughing clamour, the natives pressed around the white men till the gate was reached, and then fell back.

The girl stepped forward, and taking the trader's hand, bent her forehead to it in token of submission.

"The key of this thy house, Tāmu," she murmured in the native tongue, as she placed it in his hand.

"Enter thou first, Loisé," and he waved it away.

A faint smile of pleasure illumined her face; Baldwin, rough and careless as he was, was yet studious to observe native custom.

The white men followed her, and then in the open doorway Baldwin stopped, turned, and raised his hand, palm outwards, to the throng of natives without.

"I thank thee, friends, for thy welcome. Dear to mine ears is the sound of the tongue of the men of Rikitea. See ye this young man here. He is the son of my friend who is now dead—he whom some of ye have seen, Kapeni Paraisi" (Captain Brice).

A tall, broad-shouldered native, with his hair streaming down over his shoulders, strode up the steps, and taking the young man's hand in his, placed it to his forehead.

"The son of Paraisi is welcome to Rikitea, and to me, the chief of Rikitea."

There was a murmur of approval; Baldwin waved his hand again, and then, with Brice, entered the house.

. . . . .

Outside, the boy and girl, seated on the verandah steps, talked and waited for orders.

Said Maturei, "Loisé, think you that now Tāmu hath found thee to be faithful to his house and his name that he will marry thee according to the promise made to the priests at Tenararo when he first brought thee here?"

She took a thick coil of her shining black hair and wound it round and round her hand meditatively, looking out absently over the calm waters of the harbour.

"Who knows, Maturei? And I, I care not. Yet do I think it will be so; for what other girl is there here that knoweth his ways, and the ways of the white men as I know them? And this old man is a glutton; and, so that my skill in baking pigeons and making *karri* and rice fail me not, then am I mistress here. . . . Maturei, is not the stranger an evil-looking man?"

"Evil-looking!" said the boy, wonderingly; "nay, how canst thou say that of him?"

.   .   .   .   .

"What a jolly old fellow he is, and how these people adore him!" thought Brice, as they sat down to dinner. Two or three of the village girls waited upon them, and in the open doorway sat a vision of loveliness, arrayed in yellow muslin, and directing the movements of the girls by almost imperceptible motions of her palm-leaf fan.

Brice was strangely excited. The novelty of the surroundings, the wondrous, bright beauty of sea, and shore, and palm-grove that lay within his range of vision were already beginning to weave their fatal spell upon his susceptible nature. And then, again and again, his glance would fall upon the sweet, oval face and scarlet lips of the girl that sat in the doorway. Who was she? Not old Baldwin's wife, surely! for had not the old fellow often told him that he was not married? . . . And what a lovely spot to live in, this Rikitea! By Jove, he would like to stay a year here instead of a few months only. . . . Again his eyes rested on the figure in the doorway—and then his veins thrilled—Loisé, lazily lifting her long, sweeping lashes had caught his admiring glance.

.   .   .   .   .

Brice was no fool with women—that is, he thought so, never taking into consideration that his numerous love affairs had always ended disastrously—to the woman. And his mother, good simple soul, had thought that the best means of taking her darling son away from unapproved-of female society would be a voyage to the islands with old Tom Baldwin!

Dinner was finished, and the two men were sitting out on the verandah smoking and drinking whisky, when Brice said, carelessly—

"I wonder you never married, Baldwin."

The old trader puffed at his pipe for a minute or two ere he answered—

"Did you notice that girl at all?" and he inclined his head towards the door of the sitting-room.

The young man nodded.

Then the candid Baldwin told him her history. "I can't defend my own position. I am no better than most traders—you see it is the custom here, neither is she worse than any of these half-blooded Paumotuans. If I married a native of this particular island I would only bring trouble on my head. I could not show any preference for any particular girl for a wife without raising the bitterest quarrels among some of the leading chiefs here. You see, as a matter of fact, I should have married as soon as I came here, twenty years ago; then the trouble would have been over. But I didn't. I can see my mistake now, for I am getting old pretty fast; . . . and now that the missionaries are here, and I do a lot of business with them, I think us white men ought to show them some kind of respect by getting married—properly married —to our wives."

Brice laughed. "You mean, Baldwin, they should get married according to the rites of the Roman Catholic Church?"

"Aye," the old trader assented. "Now, there's Loisé, there—a clever, intelligent, well-educated girl, and as far as money or trade goes, as honest as the day. Can I, an old white-headed fool of sixty, go to Australia and ask any *good* woman to marry me, and come and live down here? No."

He smoked in silence awhile, and then resumed.

"Yes; honest and trustworthy she is, I believe; although the white blood in her veins is no recommendation. If ever you should live in the islands, my lad—which isn't likely—take an old fool's advice and never marry a half-caste, either in native fashion or in a church with a brass band and a bishop as leading features of the show."

. . . . .

Loisé came to them. "Will you take coffee, Tāmu?" she asked, standing before them with folded hands.

The trader bent his head, and as the girl with noiseless step glided gracefully away again he watched her.

"I think I will marry her, Brice. Sometimes when the old Marist priest comes here he makes me feel d——d uncomfortable. Of course he is too much of a gentleman—although he is a sky-pilot—to say all he would like to say, but every time he bids me good-bye he says—cunning old chap—'And think, M. Baldwin, her father, bad as he was, was a *white man.*'"

The young man listened in silence.

"I don't think I will ever go back to civilisation again, my lad—I am no use there. Here I am somebody—there I am nobody; so I think I'll give the old Father a bit of a surprise soon." Then with his merry, chuckling laugh—"and you'll be my best man. You see, it won't make any difference to you. Nearly all that I have, when I peg out, will go to you—the son of my old friend and shipmate."

A curious feeling shot through Brice's heart as he murmured his thanks. The recital of the girl's history made him burn with hot anger against her. He had thought her so innocent. And yet the old trader's words, "I've almost made up my mind to marry her," seemed to dash to the ground some vague hope, he knew not what.

. . . . .

That night he lay on a soft mat on Baldwin's verandah and tried to sleep. But from between the grey-reds of the serried line of palms that encompassed the house on all but the seaward side, a pale face with star-like eyes and ruby lips looked out and smiled upon him; in the distant and ever varying cadences of the breaking surf he heard the sweet melody of her voice;

in the dazzling brilliancy of the starry heavens her haunting face, with eyes alight with love, looked into his.

"D——n!" He rose from his couch, opened the gate, and went out along the white dazzle of the star-lit beach. "What the devil is the matter with me? I must be drunk—on two or three nips of whisky. . . . What a glorious, heavenly night! . . . And what a grand old fellow Baldwin is! . . . And I'm an infernal scoundrel to think of her—or a d——d idiot, or a miserable combination of both."

．　　．　　．　　．　　．

In a few days two things had happened. Baldwin had married Loisé, and Brice was madly in love with her and she with him. Yet scarcely a word had passed between them—he silent because of genuine shame at the treachery of his thoughts to the old man; she because she but bided her time.

One day he accepted an invitation from the old French priest to pay a visit to the Mission. He went away quietly one morning, and then wrote to Baldwin.

"Ten miles is a good long way off," he thought. "I'll be all right in a week or so—then I'll come back and be a fool no longer."

The priest liked the young man, and in his simple, hospitable way, made much of him. On the evening of the third day, as they paced to and fro on the path in the Mission garden, they saw Baldwin's boat sail up to the beach.

"See," said the priest, with a smile, "M. Baldwin will not let me keep you; and Loisé comes with him. So, so, you must go, but you will come again?" and he pressed the young Englishman's hand.

The sturdy figure of the old trader came up through the garden; Loisé, native fashion, walking behind him.

Knitting his heavy white eyebrows in mock anger he ordered Brice to the boat, and then extending his hand to the priest—" I must take him back, Father; the *Malolo* sails to-morrow, and the skipper is coming ashore to-night to dinner, to say good-bye; and, as you know, Father, I'm a silly old man with the whisky bottle, and I'll get Mr. Brice to keep me steady."

The tall, thin old priest raised his finger warningly and shook his head at old Baldwin and then smiled.

" Ah, M. Baldwin, I am very much afraid that I will never make you to understand that too much of the whisky is very bad for the head."

With a parting glass of wine they bade the good Father good-bye, and then hoisting the sail, they stood across for Rikitea. The sun had dipped, and the land-breeze stole softly down from the mountains and sped the boat along. Baldwin was noisy and jocular; Brice silent and ill at ease.

Another hour's run and Baldwin sailed the boat close under the trading schooner's stern. Leaning over the rail was the pyjama-clad captain, smoking a cigar.

" Now then, Harding," bawled the old trader, " don't forget to be up to time, eight o'clock."

" Come aboard, and make out your order for your trade, you noisy old *Areoi* devil," said Harding. " You'll 'make it out ashore,' eh? No fear, I won't trust you, you careless, forgetful old dog. So just lay up alongside, and I'll take you ashore in half an hour."

"By Jupiter, I mustn't forget the order," and Baldwin, finding he could not inveigle the captain ashore just then, ran the boat alongside the schooner and stepped over her rail—"Go on, Brice, my lad. I'll soon be with you. Give him some whisky or beer, or something, Loisé, as soon as you get to the house. He looks as melancholy as a ghost."

As the boat's crew pushed off from the schooner, Brice came aft to steer, and placing his hand on the tiller it touched Loisé's. She moved aside to make room for him, and he heard his name whispered, and in the darkness he saw her lips part in a happy smile.

Then, still silent, they were pulled ashore.

. . . . .

From his end of the house he heard a soft footfall enter the big room, and then stop. She was standing by the table when, soon after, he came out of his room. At the sound of his footstep she turned the flame of the shaded lamp to its full height, and then raised her face and looked at him. There was a strange, radiant expectancy in her eyes that set his heart to beat wildly. Then he remembered her husband—his friend.

"I suppose Tom won't be long," he began, nervously, when she came over to him and placed her hand on his sleeve. The slumbrous eyes were all aglow now, and her bosom rose and fell in short, quick strokes beneath her white muslin gown.

"Why did you go away?" she said, her voice scarce raised above a whisper, yet quivering and tremulous with emotion.

He tried to look away from her, trembling himself, and not knowing what to say.

"Ah," she said, "speak to me, answer me; why don't you say something to me? I thought that once your eyes sought mine in the boat"—then as she saw him still standing awkward and silent, all her wild passion burst out—"Brice, Brice, I love you, I love you. And you, you hate me." He tried to stop her.

Her voice sank again. "Oh, yes, yes, you hate me, else why would you go away without one word to me? Baldwin has told you of—of—of something. It is all true, quite true, and I am wicked, wicked; no woman could have been worse—and you hate me."

She released her hold upon his arm, and walking over to the window leant against it and wept passionately.

He went over to her and placed his hand upon her shoulder.

"Look here, Loisé, I'm very, very sorry I ever came here in the *Malolo*"—her shaking figure seemed to shrink at the words—"for I love you too, but, Loisé—your husband was my father's oldest friend—and mine."

The oval, tear-swept face was dangerously close to his now, and set his blood racing again in all the quick, hot madness of youth.

"What is that to me?" she whispered; "I love you."

Brice shut his fists tightly and then—fatal mistake —tried to be angry and tender at the same moment.

"Ah, but Loisé, you, as well as I, know that among English people, for a man to love his friend's wife——"

Again the low whisper—"What is that to me—and you? You love me, you say. And, we are not among English people. I have my mother's heart—not a cold English heart."

"Loisé, Baldwin is my friend. He looks upon me as his son, and he trusts me—and trusts you. . . . I could never look him in the face again. . . . If he were any other man I wouldn't care, or if, if——"

She lifted her face from his shoulder. "Then you only lied to me. You don't love me!"

That made him reckless. "Love you! By God. I love you so that if you were any other man's wife but his——" He looked steadily at her and then, with gentle force, tried to take her arm from his neck.

She knew now that he was the stronger of the two, and yet wished to hear more.

"Brice, dear Brice," she bent his head down to her lips, "if Baldwin died would you marry me?"

The faintly murmured words struck him like a shot; she still holding her arms around him, watched his face.

He kissed her on the lips. "I would marry you and never go back to the world again," he answered, in the blind passion of the moment.

A hot, passionate kiss on his lips and she was gone, and Brice, with throbbing pulses and shame in his heart, took up his hat and went out upon the beach. He couldn't meet Baldwin just then. Other men's wives had never made him feel such a miserable scoundrel as did this reckless half-blood with the scarlet lips and starry eyes.

•   •   •   •   •

That night old Baldwin and the captain of the *Malolo* got thoroughly drunk in the orthodox and time-honoured Island business fashion. Brice, afraid of "making an ass of himself," was glad to get away, and took the captain on board at midnight in Baldwin's boat, and at the mate's invitation remained for breakfast.

At daylight the mate got the *Malolo* under weigh, the skipper, with aching head, sitting up in his bunk and cursing the old trader's hospitality.

When the vessel was well outside the reef, Brice bade him good-bye, and getting his boat alongside started for the shore.

'I will—I must—clear out of this," he was telling himself as the boat swept round the point of the passage on the last sweep of the ocean swell. "I can't stay under the same roof with him day after day, month after month, and not feel my folly and her weakness. But where the deuce I can get to for five months till the schooner comes back, I don't know. There's the Mission, but that is too close; the old fellow would only bring me back again in a week."

.   .   .   .   .

Suddenly a strange, weird cry pealed over the water from the native village, a cry that to him was mysterious, as well as mournful and blood-chilling.

The four natives who pulled the boat had rested on their oars the instant they heard the cry, and with alarm and deep concern depicted on their countenances were looking toward the shore.

"What is it, boys?" said Brice in English.

Before the native to whom he spoke could answer, the long, loud wailing cry again burst forth.

"Some man die," said the native who pulled stroke-oar to Brice—he was the only one who knew English.

Then Brice, following the looks of his crew, saw

that around the white paling fence that enclosed Baldwin's house was gathered a great concourse of natives, most of whom were sitting on the ground.

"Give way, boys," he said, with an instinctive feeling of fear that something dreadful had happened. In another five minutes the boat touched the sand and Brice sprang out.

Maturei alone, of all the motionless, silent crowd that gathered around the house, rose and walked down to him.

"Oh, white man, Tāmu is dead!"

. . . . .

He felt the shock terribly, and for a moment or two was motionless and nerveless. Then the prolonged wailing note of grief from a thousand throats again broke out and brought him to his senses, and with hasty step he opened the gate and went in.

With white face and shaking limbs Loisé met him at the door and endeavoured to speak, but only hollow, inarticulate sounds came from her lips, and sitting down on a cane sofa she covered her face with her robe, after the manner of the people of the island when in the presence of death.

Presently the door of Baldwin's room opened, and the white-haired old priest came out and laid his hand sympathetically on the young man's arm, and drew him aside.

He told him all in a few words. An hour before daylight Loisé and the boy Maturei had heard the old trader breathing stertorously, and ere they could raise him to a sitting position he had breathed his last.

Heart disease, the good Father said. And he was so careless a man, was M. Baldwin. And then with tears in his eyes the priest told Brice how, from the olden times when Baldwin, pretending to scoff at the efforts of the missionaries, had yet ever been their best and truest friend.

"And now he is dead, M. Brice, and had I been but a little sooner I could have closed his eyes. I was passing in my boat, hastening to take the mission letters to the *Malolo*, when I heard the *tagi* (the death wail) of the people here, and hastening ashore found he had just passed away."

Sick at heart as he was, the young man was glad of the priest's presence, and presently together they went in and looked at the still figure in the bedroom.

When they returned to the front room they found Loisé had gone.

"She was afraid to stay in the house of death," said Maturei, "and has gone to Vehaga" (a village eight miles away), "and these are her words to the Father and to the friend of Tāmu—'Naught have I taken from the house of Tāmu, and naught do I want'— and then she was gone."

The old priest nodded to Brice—"Native blood, native blood, M. Brice. Do not, I pray you, misjudge her. She only does this because she knows the village feeling against her. She does not belong to this island, and the people here resented, in a quiet way, her marriage with my old friend. She is not cruel and ungrateful as you think. It is but her way of showing these natives that she cares not to benefit by Baldwin's death. By and by we will send for her."

. . . . . .

After Baldwin had been buried and matters

arranged, Brice and the priest, and a colleague from the Mission, read the will, and Brice found himself in possession of some two or three thousand dollars in cash and as much in trade. The house at Rikitea and a thousand dollars were for Loisé.

He told the Fathers to send word over to Vehaga and tell Loisé that he only awaited her to come and take the house over from him. As for himself he would gladly accept their kind invitation to remain at the Mission as their guest till the schooner returned.

The shock of his friend's death had all but cured him of his passion, and he felt sure now of his own strength.

. . . . .

But day after day, and then week after week passed, and no word came from Vehaga, till one evening as he leant over the railing of the garden, looking out upon the gorgeous setting of the sun into the ocean, Maturei came paddling across the smooth waters or the harbour, and, drawing his canoe up on the beach, the boy approached the white man.

"See," he said, "Loisé hath sent thee this."

He unrolled a packet of broad, dried palm leaves, and taking from it a thick necklet of sweet-smelling *kurahini* buds, placed it in Brice's hand.

He knew its meaning—it was the gift of a woman to an accepted lover.

The perfume of the flowers brought back her face to him in a moment. There was a brief struggle in his mind; and then home, friends, his future prospects in the great outside world, went to the wall, and the half-blood had won.

Slowly he raised the token and placed it over his head and round his neck.

.   .   .   .   .

In the morning she came. He held out his hand and drew her to him, and looking down into her eyes, he kissed her. Her lips quivered a little, and then the long lashes fell, and he felt her tremble.

"Loisé," he said simply, "will you be my wife?"

She glanced up at him, fearfully.

"Would you *marry* me?"

His face crimsoned—"Yes, of course. You were his wife. I can't forget that. And, besides, you said once that you loved me."

.   .   .   .   .

They were very happy for five or six years down there in Rikitea. They had one child born to them—a girl with a face as beautiful as her mother's.

Then a strange and deadly epidemic, unknown to the people of Rikitea, swept through the Paumotu Group, from Pitcairn Island to Marutea, and in every village, on every palm-clad atoll, death stalked, and the brown people sickened and shivered under their mat coverings, and died. And from island to island, borne on the very breath of the trade-wind, the terror passed, and left behind it empty, silent clusters of houses, nestling under the cocoanuts; and many a whale-ship beating back to the coast of South America, sailed close in to the shore and waited for the canoes to come off with fruit and vegetables; but none came, for the canoes had long months before blistered and cracked and rotted under the fierce rays of the Paumotu sun, and the owners lay dead in their thatched houses; for how could the dead bury the dead?

It came to Rikitea, and Harry Brice and the priests of the Mission went from village to village trying by such means as lay in their power to allay the deadly scourge. Brice had seen his little girl die, and then Loisé was smitten, and in a few days Brice saw the imprint of death stamped upon her features.

· · · · ·

As he sat and watched by her at night, and listened to the wild, delirious words of the fierce fever that held her in its cruel grasp, he heard her say that which chilled his very heart's blood. At first he thought it to be but the strange imaginings of her weak and fevered brain. But as the night wore on he was undeceived.

Just as daylight began to shoot its streaks of red and gold through the plumed palm-tops, she awoke from a fitful and tortured slumber, and opened her eyes to gaze upon the haggard features of her husband.

"Loisé," he said, with a choking voice, "tell me, for God's sake, the truth about Baldwin. *Did you kill him?*"

She put her thin, wasted hands over her dark, burning eyes, and Brice saw the tears run down and wet the pillow.

Then she answered—

"Yes, I killed him; for I loved you, and that night I went mad!"

· · · · ·

"Don't go away from me, Harry," she said, with hard, panting breaths; "don't let me die by myself.... I will soon be dead now; come closer to me, I will tell you all."

He knelt beside her and listened. She told him all in a few words. As Baldwin lay in his drunken sleep, she and Maturei had pierced him to the heart with one of the long, slender, steel needles used by the natives in mat-making. There was no blood to be seen in the morning, Maturei was too cunning for that.

Brice staggered to his feet and tried to curse her. The last grey pallor had deepened on her lips, and they moved and murmured, "It was because I loved you, Harry."

． ． ． ． ．

The sun was over the tops of the cocoanuts when the gate opened, and the white-haired old priest came in and laid his hand gently on Brice who sat with bowed figure and hidden face.

"How is your wife now, my good friend?" he asked.

Slowly the trader raised his face, and his voice sounded like a sob.

"Dead; thank God!"

With softened tread the old man passed through to the inner room, and taking the cold hands of Brice's wife tenderly within his own, he clasped them together and placed the emblem of Christ upon the quiet bosom.

AT A KAVA-DRINKING

At a Kava-Drinking.

THE first cool breaths of the land breeze, chilled by its passage through the dew-laden forest, touched our cheeks softly that night as we sat on the traders' verandah, facing the white, shimmering beach, smoking and watching the native children at play, and listening for the first deep boom of the wooden *logo* or bell that would send them racing homewards to their parents and evening prayer.

. . . . .

"There it is," said our host, who sat in the farthest corner, with his long legs resting by the heels on the white railing; "and now you'll see them scatter."

The loud cries and shrill laughter came to a sudden stop as the boom of the *logo* reached the players, and then a clear, boyish voice reached us—"*Ua ta le logo*" (the bell has sounded). Like smoke before the gale the lithe, half-naked figures fled silently in twos and threes between the cocoanuts, and the beach lay deserted.

. . . . .

One by one the lights gleamed brightly through the trees as the women piled the fires in each house with broken cocoanut shells. There was but the faintest breath of wind, and through the open sides of most of the houses not enough to flicker the steady light, as the head of the family seated himself (or herself) close to the fire, and, hymn-book in hand, led off the singing. Quite near us was a more pretentious-looking structure than the others, and looking down upon it we saw that the gravelled floor was covered with fine, clean mats, and arranged all round the sides of the house were a number of camphorwood boxes, always—in a Samoan house—the outward and visible sign of a well-to-do man. There was no fire lighted here; placed in the centre of the one room there stood a lamp with a gorgeous-looking shade, of many colours. This was the chief's house, and the chief of Aleipata was one of the strong men of Samoa—both politically and physically. Two of our party on the verandah were strangers to Samoa, and they drew their chairs nearer, and gazed with interest at the chief and his immediate following as they proceeded with their simple service. There were quite a number of the *aua-luma* (unmarried women) of the village present in the chief's house that evening, and as their tuneful voices blend in an evening hymn—" *Matou te nau e faafetai* "—we wished that instead of four verses there had been ten.

" Can you tell us, Lester," said one of the strangers to our host, " the meaning of the last words ?—they came out so clearly that I believe I've caught them," and to our surprise he sang the last line—

Ia matou moe tau ia te oe.

. . . . .

"Well, now, I don't know if I can. Samoan hymns

puzzle me; you see the language used in addressing the Deity is vastly different to that used ordinarily, but I take it that the words you so correctly repeated mean, 'Let us sleep in peace with Thee.' Curious people these Samoans," he muttered, more to himself than for us: "soon be as hypocritical as the average white man. 'Let us sleep in peace with Thee,' and that fellow (the chief), his two brothers, and about a paddockful of young Samoan bucks haven't slept at all for this two weeks. All the night is spent in counting cartridges, melting lead for bullets, and cleaning their arms, only knocking off for a drink of kava. Well, I suppose," he continued, turning to us, "they're all itching to fight, and as soon as the U.S.S. *Resacca* leaves Apia they'll commence in earnest, and us poor devils of traders will be left here doing nothing and cursing this infernal love of fighting, which is inborn with Samoans and a part of their natural cussedness which, if the Creator hadn't given it to them, would have put many a dollar into my pocket."

. . . . .

"Father," said a voice that came up to us from the gloom of the young cocoanuts' foliage at the side of the house, "Felipe is here, and wants to know if he may come up and speak to the *alii papalagi* (white gentlemen)."

"Right you are, Felipe, my lad," said the trader in a more than usual kindly voice, "bring him up, Atalina, and then run away to the chief's and get some of the *aua-luma* to come over with you and make a bowl of kava."

"Now, Doctor L——," Lester continued, addressing himself to one of his guests, the surgeon of an

American war vessel then stationed in Samoa, and a fellow-countryman of his, " I'll show you as fine a specimen of manhood and intelligence as God ever made, although he has got a tanned hide."

. . . . .

The native that ascended the steps and stood before us with his hat in his hand respectfully saluting, was indeed, as Lester called him, "a fine specimen." Clothed only in a blue and white *lava lava* or waist-cloth, his clean-cut limbs, muscular figure, and skin like polished bronze, stood revealed in the full light that now flooded room and verandah from the lamp lit in the sitting-room. The finely-plaited Manhiki hat held in his right hand seemed somewhat out of place with the rest of his attire, and was evidently not much worn. Probably Felipe had merely brought it for the occasion, as a symbol to us of his superior tastes and ideas.

He shook hands with us all round, and then, at Lester's invitation, followed us inside, and sat down cross-legged on the mats and courteously awaited us to talk to him. The American surgeon offered him a cigar, which he politely declined, and produced from the folds of his *lava lava* a bundle of banana-leaf cigarettes, filled with strong tobacco. One of these, at a nod from the trader, he lit, and commenced to smoke.

. . . . .

In a few minutes we heard the crunching of the gravelled path under bare feet, and then some three or four of the *aua-luma*—the kava-chewing girls—ascended the steps and took up their position by the huge wooden kava bowl. As the girls, under the careful supervision of the trader's wife, prepared the drink, we fell into a general conversation.

"I wonder now," said the doctor to the trader, "that you, Lester, who, by your own showing, are by no means infatuated with the dreamy monotony of island life, can yet stay here, year after year, seeing nothing and hearing nothing of the world that lies outside these lonely islands. Have you no desire at all to go back again into the world?"

A faint movement—the index of some rapidly passing emotion—for a moment disturbed the calm, placid features of Lester, as he answered quietly: "No, doctor, I don't think it's likely I'll ever see the outside world, as you call it, again. I've had my hopes and ambitions, like every one else; but they didn't pan out as I expected, . . . and then I became Lester the Trader, and as Lester the Trader I'll die, have a whitey-brown crowd at my funeral; and, if you came here ten years afterwards, the people couldn't even tell you where I was planted."

The doctor nodded. "Just so. Like all native races, their affections and emotions are deep but transient—no better in that way than the average American nigger."

The kava was finished now, and was handed round to us by the slender graceful hands of the trader's little daughter. As Felipe, the last to drink, handed back the *ipu* to the girl, his eyes lit up, and he spoke to our host, addressing him, native fashion, by his Christian name, and speaking in his own tongue.

"How is it, Tiaki (Jack), that I hear thee tell these thy friends that we of the brown skins have but shallow hearts and forget quickly? Dost think that if, when thy time comes, and thou goest, that thy wife and child will not grieve? Hast thou not heard of our white man who, when he died, yet left his name upon our hearts?—and yet we were in those days heathens and followers of our own gods."

The trader nodded kindly, and turned to us. "Do you want to hear a yarn about one of the old style of white men that used to live like fighting-cocks in Samoa? Felipe here has rounded on me for saying that his countrymen soon forget, and has brought up this wandering *papalagi tafea* (beachcomber) as an instance of how the natives will stick to a man once he proves himself a man."

II.

"It was the tenth year after the Cruel Captain with the three ships had anchored in Apia,[1] and when we of Aleipata were at war with the people of Fagaloa. In those days we had no white man in this town and longed greatly to get one. But they were few in Samoa then; one was there at Tiavea, who had fled from a man-of-war of England, one at Saluafata, and perhaps one or two more at Tutuila or Savaii—that was all.

"My father's name was Lauati. He, with his mother, lived on the far side of the village, away from the rest of the houses. There were no others living in the house with them, for my father's mother was very poor, and all day long she laboured—some-

---

[1] Commodore Wilkes, in command of the famous United States Exploring Expedition, 1836-40. He was a noted martinet, and was called *Le alii Saua* (the Cruel Captain).

times at making mats, and sometimes at beating out *siapo* (tappa) cloth. As the mats were made, and the tappa was bleached, and figures and patterns drawn upon it, she rolled them up and put them away overhead on the beams of the house, for she was eaten up with poverty, and these mats and tappa cloth was she gathering together so that she might be able to pay for my father's tattooing. And as she worked on the shore, so did my father toil on the sea, for although he was not yet tattooed he was skilled more than any other youth in *sisu atu* (bonita catching). Sometimes the chief, who was a greedy man, would take all his fish and leave him none for himself to take home to his house. Sometimes he would give him one, and then my father would cut off a piece for his mother, and take the rest and sell it for taro and bread-fruit. And all this time he worked, worked with his mother, so that he would have enough to pay for his tattooing, for to reach his age and not be tattooed is thought a disgrace.

．　　　．　　　．　　　．　　　．

" Now, in the chief's house was a young girl named Uluvao. She used to meet my father by stealth, for the chief—who was her uncle—designed to give her in marriage to a man of Siumu, who was a little chief, and had asked him for her. So Uluvao, who dreaded her uncle's wrath, would creep out at night from his house, and going down to the beach swim along the shore till she came to the lonely place where my father lived. His mother would await her coming on the beach, and then these three would sit together in the house and talk. If a footstep sounded, then the girl would flee, for she knew her uncle's club would soon bite into my father's brain did he know of these stolen meetings.

. . . . .

"One day it came about that a great *fono* (meeting) was to be held at Falealili, and Tuialo, the chief, and many other chiefs, and their *tulafale*, or talking men, set out to cross the mountains to Falealili. Six days would they be away, and Uluvao and my father rejoiced, for they could now meet and speak openly, for the fear of the chief's face was not before them, and the people of the village knew my father loved the girl, so when they saw them together they only smiled, or else turned their faces another way. That night, in the big council house, there was a great number of the young men and women gathered together, and they danced and sang, and much kava was drunk. Presently the sister of the chief, who was a woman with a bitter tongue, came to the house, and saw and mocked at my father, and called him a 'naked wretch.' (Thou knowest, Tiaki, if a man be not tattooed we called him naked.)

"'Alas!' said my father, 'I am poor; oh, lady, how can I help it?'

"The old woman's heart softened. 'Get thee out upon the sea and catch a fat turtle for a gift to my brother, and thou shalt be tattooed when he returns,' she said.

"The people laughed, for they knew that turtle were not to be caught at a silly woman's bidding. But my father rose up and went out into the darkness towards his house. As he walked on the sand his name was called, and Uluvao ran by his side.

"'Lauati,' she said, 'let me come with thee. Let

us hasten and get thy canoe, and seek a turtle on Nu'ulua and Nu'utele, for the night is dark, and we may find one.'

"My father took her hand, and they ran and launched the canoe.

. . . . .

"My father paddled, Uluvao sat in the bow of the canoe. The night was very dark, and she was frightened, for in the waters hereabout are many *tanifa*, the thick, short shark, that will leap out of the water and fall on a canoe and crush it, so that those who paddle may be thrown out and devoured. And as she trembled she looked out at the shore of the two islands, which were now close to, and said to my father, 'Lo! what is this? I see a light as of a little fire.'

"Lauati ceased to paddle and looked. And there, between the trunks of the cocoanuts, he saw the faint gleam of a little fire, and something, as of a figure, that moved.

"The girl Uluvao had a quick wisdom. 'Ah,' said she, 'perhaps it is the war canoes (taumualua) from Falifa. Those dogs hath learnt that all our men are gone away to Falealili to the *fono*, and they have come here to the islands to eat and rest, so that they may fall upon our town when it is dawn, and slay us all. Let us back, ere it is too late.'

"But as she spoke she looked into the water, and my father looked too; and they both trembled. Deep down in the blackness of the sea was it that they saw—yet it quickly came nearer and nearer, like unto a great flame of white fire. It was a *tanifa*. Like flashes of lightning did my father dash his paddle into the water and urge the canoe to the land, for he knew that when the *tanifa* had come to the surface it would look and then dive, and when it came up again would spring upon and devour them both.

"'It is better to give our heads to the men of Falifa than for us to go into the belly of the shark,' he said, 'and it may be we can land, and they see us not.' And so with fear gnawing at their vitals the canoe flew along, and the streak of fire underneath was close upon them when they struck the edge of the coral and knew they were safe.

· · · · ·

"They dragged the canoe over the reef and then got in again, and paddled softly along till they passed the light of the fire, and then they landed on a little beach about a hundred *gafa* (fathoms) away. Then again Uluvao, who was a girl of wisdom, spoke.

· · · · ·

"'Listen,' she said, 'O man of my heart. Let us creep through the bushes and look. It may be that these men of Falifa are tired and weary, and sleep like hogs. Take thou, then, O Lauati, thy shark club and knife from the canoe, and perchance we may fall upon one that sleepest away from the rest, then shalt thou strike, and thou and I drag him away into the bushes and take his head. Then, ere it is well dawn, we will be back in the town, and Tuialo will no longer keep me from thee, for the head of a Falifa man will win his heart better than a fat turtle, and I will be wife to thee.'

"My father was pleased at her words. So they crept like snakes along the dewy ground. When they came to a jagged boulder covered with vines, that was near unto the fire, they looked and saw but one man, and, lo! he was a *papalagi*—a white man. And then, until it was dawn, my father and the girl hid behind the jagged rock and watched.

. . . . .

"The white man was sitting on the sand, with his face clasped in his hands. At his feet lay another man, with his white face turned up to the sky, and those that watched saw that he was dead. He who sat over the dead man was tall and thin, and his hands were like the talons of the great fish eagle, so thin and bony were they. His garments were ragged and old, and his feet were bare; and as my father looked at him his heart became pitiful, and he whispered to Uluvao, 'Let us call out. He is but weak, and I can master him if he springs upon me. Let us speak.'

"But Uluvao held him back. 'Nay,' she said, 'he may have a gun and shoot.'

"So they waited till the sun rose.

. . . . .

"The white man stood and looked about. Then he walked down to the beach, and my father and the girl saw lying on the rocks a little boat. The man went to the side, and put in his hand and brought out something in his hand, and came back and sat down again by the face of the dead. He had gone to the boat for food, and my father saw him place a biscuit to his mouth and commence to eat. But ere he swallowed any it fell from his hand upon the sand and he threw himself upon the body of the dead man and wept, and his tears ran down over the face that was cold and were drank up by the sand.

"Then Uluvao began to weep, and my father stood up and called out to the white man *Talofa!*

"He gazed at them and spoke not, but let them come close to him, and pointing to him who lay on the sand, he covered his face with his hands and bowed his head. Then Lauati ran and climbed a cocoanut tree and brought him two young nuts and made him drink, and Uluvao got broad leaves and covered over the face of the dead from the hot sun. Not one word of our tongue could he speak, but yet from signs that he made Lauati and the girl knew that he wished to bury the dead man. So they two dug a deep grave in the sand, far up on the bank, where it lay soft and deep and covered with vines. When it was finished they lifted the dead white man and laid him beside it. And as they looked upon him the other came and knelt beside it and spoke many words into the ear that heard not, and Uluvao wept again to see his grief. At last they laid him in the grave and all three threw in the sand and filled it up.

"Then these two took the strange white man by the hand and led him away into a little hut that was sometimes used by those who came to the island to fish. They made him eat and then sleep, and while he slept they carried up the things out of the boat and put them in the house beside him.

. . . . .

"When the sun was high in the heavens, the white man awoke, and my father took his hand and pointed to the boat, and then to the houses across the sea. He bent his head and followed, and they all got into the boat, and hoisted the sail. When the boat came close to the passage of Aleipata, the people ran from out their houses, and stood upon the beach and wondered. And Lauati and Uluvao laughed and sang, and called out: 'Ho, ho, people! we have brought a great gift—a white man from over the sea. Send word quickly to Tuialo that he may return and see this our white man,' and, as the boat touched the sand, the old woman, the sister of Tuialo, came up, and said to Lauati, 'Well hast thou done, O lucky one! Better is this gift of a white man than many turtle.'

"Then she took the stranger to her house, and pigs and fowls were killed, and yams and taro cooked, and a messenger sent to Tuialo to hasten back quickly, and see this gift from the gods. For they were quick to see that in the boat were muskets and powder and bullets, and all the people rejoiced, for they thought that this white man could mend for them many guns that were broken and useless, and help them to fight against the men ot Falifa.

 . . . . .

"In two days Tuialo came back, and he made much of the white man, and Uluvao he gave to my father for wife. And for the white man were the softest mats and the best pieces of *siapo*, and he lived for nearly the space of two years in the chief's house. And all this time he worked at making boats and mending the broken guns and muskets, and little by little the words of our tongue came to him, and he learned to tell us many things. Yet at night-time he would always come to my father's house and sit with him and talk, and sometimes Uluvao would make kava for him and my father.

"At about the end of the second year, there came a

whaleship, and Tuialo, and the white man, whom we called *Tui-fana*, 'the gun-mender,' went out to her, and took with them many pigs and yams to exchange for guns and powder. When the buying and selling was over, the captain of the ship gave Tui-fana a gun with two barrels—bright was it and new, and Tuialo, the chief, was eaten up with envy, and begged his white man for the gun, but he said: 'Nay, not now; when we are in the house we will talk.'

. . . . .

"Like as a swarm of flies, the people gathered round the council-house to see the guns and the powder and the swords that had been brought from the ship. And in the middle of the house sat Tui-fana with the gun with two barrels in his hand.

"When all the chiefs had come in and sat down Tuialo came. His face was smiles, but his heart was full of bitterness towards Tui-fana, and as he spoke to the people and told them of the words that had been spoken by the captain of the ship, he said, 'And see this white man, this Tui-fana, who hath grown rich among us, is as greedy as a Tongan, and keepeth for himself a new gun with two barrels.'

"The white stood up and spoke: 'Nay, not greedy am I. Take, O chief, all I have; my house, my mats, my land, and the wife thou gavest me, but yet would I say, "Let me keep this gun with the two barrels."'

"Tuialo was eaten up with greed, yet was his mind set on the gun, so he answered, 'Nay, that were to make thee as poor as when thou comest to us. Give me the gun, 'tis all I ask.'

"'It is not mine to give,' he answered. Then he

rose and spoke to the people. 'See,' said he, 'Tuialo, the chief, desires this gun, and I say it is not mine to give, for to Lauati did I promise such a gun a year gone by. This, then, will I do. Unto Tuialo will I give my land, my house, and all that is mine, but to Lauati I give the gun, for so I promised.'

. . . . .

"Then fierce looks passed between the chief and the white man, and the people surged together to and fro, for they were divided, some for the fear of the chief, and some for the love of the white man. But most were for that Lauati should keep the gun. And so Tuialo, seeing that the people's hearts were against him, put on a smooth face, and came to the white man and said—

"'Thou art as a son to me. Lauati shall keep the gun, and thou shalt keep thy house and lands. I will take nothing from thee. Let us be for ever friends.'

"Then the white said to the chief, 'O chief, gladly will I give thee all I have, but this man, Lauati, is as my brother, and I promised——'

"But Tuialo put his hand on the white man's mouth, and said, 'Say no more, my son; I was but angered.'

. . . . .

"Yet see now his wickedness. For that night, when my father and Uluvao, my mother, were sitting with the white man and his wife, and drinking kava, there suddenly sprang in upon them ten men, who stood over them with clubs poised. They were the body-men of Tuialo.

"'Drink thy kava,' said one to the white man, 'and then come out to die.'

. . . . .

"Ah, he was a man! He took the cup of kava from the hands of his wife's sister, and said—

"'It is well. All men must die. But yet would I see Tuialo before the club falls.'

"The chief but waited outside, and he came.

"'Must I die?' said the white man.

"'Ay,' said Tuialo. 'Two such as thee and I cannot live at the same time. Thou art almost as great a man as I.'

"The white man bent his head. Then he put out his hand to my father and said, 'Farewell, O my friend.'

"Lauati, my father, fell at the chief's feet. 'Take thou the gun, O chief, but spare his life.'

"Tuialo laughed. 'The gun will I take, Lauati, but his life I must have also.'

"'My life for his,' said my father.

"'And mine,' said Uluvao, my mother.

"'And mine also,' said Manini, the white man's wife; and both she and Taulaga, her sister, bent their knees to the chief.

"The white man tried to spring up, but four strong men held him.

"Then Tuialo looked at the pair who knelt before him. He stroked his club, and spoke to his body-men.

"'Bring them all outside.' They went together to the beach. 'Brave talkers ye be,' said he; 'who now will say "I die for the white man"?'

"'Nay, heed them not, Tuialo,' said the white man. 'On me alone let the club fall.'

"But the chief gave him no answer, looking only at my father and the three women.

．　　．　　．　　．　　．

"'My life,' said Taulaga, the girl; and she knelt on the sand.

"The club swung round and struck her on the side of her head, and it beat it in. She fell, and died quickly.

"'Oho,' mocked Tuialo, 'is there but one life offered for so great a man as Tiufana?'

"Lauati fell before him. 'Spare me not, O chief, if my life but saves his.'

"And again the club swung, and Lauati, my father, died too, and as he fell his blood mixed with that of Taulaga.

"And then Uluvao and Manini, placing some little faith in his mocking words, knelt, and their blood too poured out on the ground, and the three women and my father lay in a heap together.

"Now I, Felipe, was but a child, and when my mother had gone to kneel under the club she had placed me under a *fetan* tree near by. The chief's eye fell on me, and a man took me up and carried me to him.

"Then the white man said, 'Hurt not the child, O chief, or I curse thee before I die, and thou wastest away.'

"So Tuialo spared me.

"Then the chief came to the white man, and the two who held his hands pulled them well apart, and Tuialo once more swung his blood-dyed club. It fell, and the white man's head fell upon his breast."

MRS. LIARDET: A SOUTH SEA TRADING EPISODE

Mrs. Liardet: a South Sea Trading Episode.

CAPTAIN DAVE LIARDET, of the trading schooner *Motutakea*, of Sydney, was sitting propped up in his bunk smoking his last pipe. His very last.. He knew that, for the Belgian doctor-naturalist, his passenger, had just said so ; and besides, one look at the gaping hole in his right side, that he had got two days before at La Vandola, in the Admiralties, from the broad-bladed obsidian native knife, had told him he had made his last voyage. The knife-blade lay on the cabin table before him, and his eye rested on it for a moment with a transient gleam of satisfaction as he remembered how well Tommy, the Tonga boy, who pulled the bow oar, had sent a Snider bullet through the body of the yellow-skinned buck from whom the knife-thrust had come. From the blade of obsidian on the table his eye turned to the portrait of a woman in porcelain that hung just over the clock. It was a face fair enough to look at, and Liardet, with a muttered curse of physical agony, leant his body forward to get a closer view of it, and said, "Poor little woman ; it'll be darned rough on her." Then Russell, the mate, came down.

· · · · ·

"Joe," said Liardet, in his practical way, which even the words of the doctor and the face of the clock before him could not change, "cock your ears and listen, for I haven't got much time, and you have the ship to look to. I want you to tell the owners that this affair at La Vandola wasn't my fault. We was doing fair and square trading when a buck drives his knife into me for no apparent reason beyond the simple damned fun of the thing. Well, he's done for me, and Tommy Tonga for him, and that's all you've got to say about that. Next thing is to ask 'em to sling Tommy a fiver over and above his wages—for saving of the boat and trade, mind, Joe. Don't say for potting the nigger, Joe; boat and trade, boat and trade, that's the tack to go on with owners, Joe. Well, let's see now. . . . My old woman. See she gets fair play, wages up to date of death, eh, Joe? By God, old man, she won't get much of a cheque—only four months out now from Sydney. Look here, Joe, the Belgian's all right. He won't go telling tales. So don't you log me dead for another month, and make as bad a passage as you can. There's only us three white men aboard, and the native boys will take their Bible oath I didn't die until the ship was off Lord Howe Island if you give 'em a box of tobacco. You see, Joe? That's the dodge. More days, more dollars, and the longer you keep the ship at sea the more money comes to all hands. And I know I can trust you, Joe, to lend a hand in making the old woman's cheque a little bigger. Right. . . . We've been two years together now, Joe, and this is the only thing I've ever asked you to do or done myself that wasn't square and aboveboard. But look here"—here, for some half-minute, Captain Dave Liardet launched into profanity—"I tell you that the owners of this ship wouldn't care a single curse if you and I and every living soul aboard had had our livers cut out at La Vandola as long as *they* didn't lose money over it, and haven't to pay our wages to our wives and children."

. . . . .

Liardet gasped and choked, and the little Belgian naturalist tripped down and wiped away the dark stream that began to trickle down the grizzled beard, and then he and Russell, the mate, laid him down again.

"Don't go," whispered the Belgian to the other, "he sink ver' fast now." The closed eyelids opened a little and looked up through the skylight at the brown face of Tommy the Tongan, and then Russell gave the dying skipper brandy and water. Then, with fast-fading eyes on the picture in porcelain, he asked Russell what course he was keeping.

"As near south as can be," said the mate, "but with this breeze we could soon make the Great Barrier, and there's always hope, cap'n. Let me keep her away to the westward a bit, and who knows but you may——"

For answer the grizzled Liardet held out his hand, shook his head faintly, and muttering, "I hope to God it'll come on a Hell of a Calm for a Month of Sundays," he turned his face to the port and went over *his* Great Barrier.

. . . . .

Every one was "*so* sorry for poor little Mrs. Liardet." She was so young to be a widow, "and having no children, my dear, the poor creature must have felt the shock the more keenly." Thus the local gabble of the acquaintances and friends of the pretty widow. And she laughed softly to herself that she couldn't feel overwhelmed with grief at her widowhood. "He hadn't a thought above making money," she said to herself—oh, Nell Liardet, for whom did he desire to make it!—"and yet never could make it." And then she thought of Russell, and smiled again. His hand had trembled when it held hers. Surely he did not come so often to see her merely to talk of rough, old Dave Liardet. A man whom she had only tolerated—never loved. And then, Russell was a big, handsome man; and she liked big, handsome men. Also, he was captain now. And, of course, when he had told her of that rich patch of pearl-shell, that he alone knew of at Caillê Harbour, in which was a small fortune, and had looked so intently into her blue eyes, he had meant that it was for her. "Yes," and she smiled again, "I'm sure he loves me. But he's terribly slow; and although I do believe that blonde young widows look 'fetching' in black, I'm getting sick of it, and wish he'd marry me to-morrow."

. . . . .

Russell had stood to his compact with the dead skipper. The owners had given her £150, and Russell, making up a plausible story to his dead captain's wife of Liardet having in bygone days lent him "fifty pounds," had added that sum to the other. And he meant, for the sake of old Dave, never to let his pretty little widow run short as long as he had a shot in the locker. The patch of shell at Caillê he meant to work, and if Dave had lived they would have "gone whacks." But as he was dead, he wouldn't do any mean thing. She should have half of whatever he got—"go whacks" just the same. But as for love, it never entered his honest brain, and had any one told him that Nell Liardet was fond of him, he would have called him a liar and "plugged" him for insulting a lady.

.   .   .   .   .

"Going away! Mr. Russell—Joe! Surely you won't go and leave me without a friend in the world? I thought you cared for me more than that?"

The big man reddened up to his temples.

"Don't say that, Mrs. Liardet. If you'll allow me, I'll always be a friend. And, as I thought it would be hard for you to have to spend the little that Liardet left you, I have made arrangements for you to draw a few pounds whenever you need it from the agents. And as long as ever I have a pound in the world, Dave Liardet's wife——"

"Wife!" and the blue eyes flashed angrily. "He is dead and I am free. Why do you always talk of him? I hate the name. I hated him—a coarse, money-loving——"

"Stop!"

Russell stepped forward. "Good-bye, Mrs. Liardet. I hold to what I have said. But the man that you call coarse and money-loving died in trying to make it for you. And he was a good, honest man, and I can't stay here and hear his memory abused by the woman he loved better than life." And then he turned to go, but stopped, and, with a scarlet face, said, "Of course you're a lady and wouldn't do anything not right and straight, so I know that if you intend to marry again you'll send me word; but if you don't, why, of course, I'll be proud and glad to stand by you in money matters. I'm sure poor Dave would have done the same for my wife if I had got that knife into me instead of him."

Nell Liardet, sitting with clenched hands and set teeth, said, in a hoarse voice, "Your wife! Are you married?"

"Well—er—yes, oh, yes. I have a—er—native wife at the Anchorites. Poor old Dave stood godfather to one of my little girls. God knows how anxious I am to get back to her."

"*Good*-bye, Mr. Russell!"

KENNEDY THE BOATSTEERER

Kennedy the Boatsteerer.

STEERING north-west from Samoa for six or seven hundred miles you will sight the Ellice Group—low-lying, palm-clad coral atolls fringed on the lee with shimmering sandy beaches. On the weather-side, exposed to the long sweep of the ocean-rollers, there are but short, black-looking reefs backed by irregular piles of loose, flat, sea-worn coral, thrown up and accumulating till its surface is brushed by the pendant leaves of the cocoanuts, only to be washed and swirled back seawards when the wind comes from the westward and sends a fierce sweeping current along the white beaches and black coral rocks alike.

. . . . .

Twenty-three years ago these islands were almost unknown to any one save a few wandering traders and the ubiquitous New Bedford whaler. But now, long ere you can see from the ship's deck the snowy tumble of the surf on the reef, a huge white mass, grim, square, and ugly, will meet your eye—whitewashed walls of a distressful ghastliness accentuated by doors and windows of the deadliest black. This cheerful excrescence on the face of suffering nature is a native church.

The people have mostly assimilated themselves, in their manners and mode of life generally, to the new order of things represented by the fearful-looking structure aforementioned. That is to say, even as the Tongan and Fijian, they have degenerated from a fierce, hardy, warlike race into white-shirted, black-coated saints, whose ideal of a lovely existence is to have public prayer twice a day on week-days and all day on Sundays. To them it is a good thing to get half a dollar from the white trader for a sick fowl—which, when bought, will be claimed by another native, who will have the white man fined two dollars for buying stolen property. Had the white man paid a dollar he had done wisely—that coin sometimes goes far in the Tokelaus. For instance, the truly unctuous native Christian may ask a dollar for two fowls, but he will also lease out his wife for a similar amount. Time was, in the Ellices, when the undue complaisance of a married woman meant a sudden and inartistic compression of the jugular, or a swift blow from the heavy, ebony-wood club of the wronged man. Nowadays, since the smug-faced native teacher hath shown them the Right Way, such domestic troubles are condoned by—a dollar. That is, if it be a genuine American dollar or two British florins; for outraged honour would not accept the cast-iron Bolivian money or the poor silver of Chili and Peru. And for a dollar the native "Christian" can all but pay for a nicely-bound Bible, printed in the Samoan tongue, and thus, no doubt, out of evil would come good; for he could, by means of his newly-acquired purchase, picture to his dusky mate the terrors that await those who look upon strange men and *tupe fa'apupula* (bright and shining money).

. . . . .

But I want to tell about Kennedy. Kennedy the Boatsteerer he was called; although twenty years had passed and gone since that day at Wallis Island when he, a bright-eyed, bronze-faced lad—with the fighting-blood of the old Puritan Endicotts running like fire through his veins despite his New England bringing-up—ran his knife into a shipmate's heart and fled for ever from all white associations. Over a woman it was, and only a copper-coloured one at that; but then she was young and beautiful, with dreamy, glistening eyes, and black, wavy hair, ornamented with a wreath of orange-flowers and coil upon coil of bright-hued *seă seă* berries strung together, hanging from her neck and resting upon her dainty bosom.

. . . . .

Standing at the doorway of his house, looking over the placid waters at the rising sun, Kennedy folds his brawny arms across his bare, sun-tanned chest and mutters to himself, in his almost forgotten mother-tongue: "Twenty years, twenty years ago! Who would know me there now? Even if I placarded my name on my back and what I did, 'taint likely I'd have to face a grand jury for running a knife into a mongrel Portuguee, way out in the South Seas a score of years ago. . . . Poor little Talamălu! I paid a big price for her—twenty years of wandering from Wallis Island to the Bonins; and wherever I go that infernal story follows me up. Well, I'll risk it anyhow, and the first chance that comes along I'll cut

Kanaka life and drinking ship's rum and go see old dad and mum to home. Here, Tikena, you Tokelau devil, bring me my toddy."

A native, clad in his grass *titi*, takes from a wooden peg in the house wall two shells of toddy, and the white wanderer takes one and drinks. He is about to return the other to the man when two girls come up from the beach with their arms around each other's waists, Tahiti fashion, and one calls out with a laugh to "leave some in the shell." This is Laumanu, and if there is one thing in the world that Jake Kennedy cares for above himself it is this tall girl with the soft eyes and lithe figure. And he dreams of her pretty often, and curses fluently to think that she is beyond his reach and is never likely to fill the place of Talamălu and her many successors. For Laumanu is *tabu* to a Nuitao chief—that is, she has been betrothed, but the Nuitao man is sixty miles away at his own island, and no one knows when he will claim his *avaga*. Then the girl gives him back the empty toddy-shell, and, slyly pinching his hand, sails away with her mate, whereupon the susceptible Kennedy, furious with long disappointment, flings himself down on his bed of mats, curses his luck and his unsuspecting rival at Nuitao, and finally decides not to spring a surprise on "dad and mum" by going "hum" for a considerable number of years to come.

. . . . .

Mr. Jake Kennedy at this time was again a widower —in the widest sense of the word. The last native girl who had occupied the proud position of *Te avaga te papalagi* (the white man's wife) was a native of the island of Maraki—a dark-skinned, passionately jealous creature, who had followed his fortunes for three years to his present location, and then developed *mal-du-pays* to such an extent that the local priest and devil-catcher, one Pare-vaka, was sent for by her female attendants. Pare-vaka was not long in making his diagnosis. A little devil in the shape of an octopus was in Tenenapa's brain. And he gave instructions how to get the fiend out, and also further instructions to one of the girl attendants to fix, point-upwards, in the sick woman's mat the *foto*, or barb of the sting-ray. So when Kennedy, who, in his rough, careless way, had some faint fondness for the woman who three years ago he went mad over, heard a loud cry in the night and was told that Tenenapa was dead, he did not know that as the sick woman lay on her side the watchers had quietly turned her with her face to the roof, and with the needle pointed *foto* pierced her to the heart. And old Pare-vaka rejoiced, for he had a daughter who, in his opinion, should be *avaga* to the wealthy and clever white man, who could *tori nui* and *sisi atu* (pull cocoanuts and catch bonito) like any native; and this Tenenapa—who was she but a dog-eating stranger from Maraki only fit for shark's meat? So the people came and brought Kennedy the "gifts of affliction" to show their sympathy, and asked him to take a wife from their own people. And he asked for Laumanu.

. . . . .

There was a dead silence awhile, and then a wild-looking creature with long white hair falling around his shoulders like a cloak, dreading to shame the *papalagi* before so many, rose to his feet and motioned them away. Then he spoke: "Forget the words you have said, and take for a wife the girl from the house of Pare-vaka. Laumanu is *tabu,* and death walks behind her." But Kennedy sulked and wanted Laumanu or none.

And this is why he feels so bad to-day, and the rum-keg gives him no consolation. For the sweet-voiced Laumanu always runs away from him when he steps out from his dark little trade-room into the light, with unsteady steps and a peculiar gleam in his black eye, that means mischief—rude love to a woman and challenge to fight to a man.

Lying there on his mat, plotting how to get possession of the girl, there comes to him a faint cry, gradually swelling in volume until every voice in the village, from the full, sonorous tones of the men to the shrill treble of the children, blend together: " *Te vaka motu! Te vaka motu!* " (a ship! a ship!). Springing up, he strides out, and there, slowly lumbering round the south-west end of the little island, under cruising canvas only, he sees her. One quick glance shows her to be a whaler.

In ten minutes Kennedy is in a canoe, flying over the reef, and in as many more alongside and on deck. The captain is an old acquaintance, and while the boats are sent ashore to buy pigs and poultry, Kennedy and he have a long talk in the cabin. Then the skipper says, as he rises, "Well, it's risky, but it's a smart way of earning five hundred dollars, and I'll land you and the creature somewhere in the Carolines."

The whaler was to lie off and on all night, or until such time as Kennedy and the girl came aboard in a canoe. To avert suspicion, the captain was to remain ashore with his boat's crew to witness a dance, and, if all went well, the white man was to be aboard before him with Laumanu and stow her away, in case any canoes came off with the boat.

. . . . .

The dance was in full swing when Kennedy, stripped to the waist, with a heavy bag of money in his left hand and a knife in his right, took a long farewell of his house and stepped out into the silent groves of coco-palms. A short walk brought him to a salt lagoon. On the brink he stood and waited, until a trembling, voiceless figure joined him from out the depths of the thick mangroves. Hand-in-hand they fled along the narrow, sandy path till they reached the beach, just where a few untenanted thatched huts stood on the shingle. Between these, covered over with cocoanut branches, lay a canoe. Deftly the two raised the light craft and carried it down to the water that broke in tender, rippling murmurs on the white sand. And with Laumanu seated for'ard, gazing out beyond into the blackness before them, he urged the canoe seawards with quick, nervous strokes. Far away to the westward he could see the dull glimmer of the whaleship's lights.

. . . . .

The mate of the *Essex* was leaning over the rail, drowsily watching the phosphorescence in the water as the ship rolled gently to the ocean swell, when a cry came from for'ard: "A heavy squall coming down, sir, from the land!" And it did come, with a swift, fierce rush, and so strong that it nearly threw the old whaler over on her beam-ends. In the midst of the hum and roar of the squall some one in the waist of the ship called out something about a canoe being alongside. The mate's comment was brief but vigorous, and the matter was speedily forgotten. Then the rain fell in torrents, and as the ship was made snug the watch got under shelter and the mate went below to get a drink of rum, and curse his captain for loafing ashore, watching naked women dancing.

· · · · ·

Three miles further out a canoe was drifting and tossing about with outrigger carried away. Now and then, as a big sea lifted her, the stern would rise high out of the water and the sharp-nosed whaleback for'ard go down as if weighted heavily. And it was—with a bag of dollars lashed underneath. When in the early morning the whaleship sighted the drifting speck, floating on the bosom of a now placid sea, the thoughtful Down-East skipper—observant of the canoe's bows being under water—lowered a boat and pulled over to it. He took the bag of dollars and muttering something about "rather thinking he was kinder acquainted with the poor man's people," went back to the ship and stood away on his course in pursuit of his greasy vocation.

· · · · ·

And Kennedy and the girl! Go some night and watch the dark-skinned people catching flying-fish by the light of *au lama* torches. Look over the side of the canoe and see those swarms of grim, grey devils of the tropic seas that ever and anon dart to the surface as the paddlers' hands come perilously near the water, and wonder no longer as to the fate of Kennedy the Boatsteerer and his Laumanu.

A DEAD LOSS

A Dead Loss.

DENISON, the supercargo of the *Indiana*, was sent by his " owners " to an island in the S.W. Pacific where they had a trading business, the man in charge or which had, it was believed, got into trouble by shooting a native. His instructions were to investigate the rumour, and, if the business was suffering in any way, to take away the trader and put another man in his place. The incident here related is well within the memory of some very worthy men who still dwell under the roofs of thatch in the Western Pacific.

.   .   .   .   .

The name of the island was—well, say Nukupapau. The *Indiana* sailed from Auckland in December, and made a smart run till the blue peaks of Tutuila were sighted, when the trades failed and heavy weather came on from the westward. Up to this time Denison's duties as supercargo had kept him busy in the trade-room, and he had had no time to study his new captain, for, although they met at table three times a day, beyond a few civilities they had done no talking. Captain Chaplin was young—about thirty—and one of the most taciturn persons Denison had ever met. The mate, who, having served the owners for about twenty years, felt himself privileged, one night at supper asked him point-blank, in his Irish fashion *apropos* of nothing: "An' phwat part av the wurruld may yez come from, captain?"

There were but the five of them present—the skipper, two mates, boatswain, and Denison. Laying down his knife and fork and stirring his tea, he fixed his eyes coldly on the inquisitive sub's face.

"From the same God-forsaken hole as you do, sir—Ireland. My name isn't Chaplin, but as I'm the captain of this rotten old hooker I want you to understand that if you ask me another such d——d impertinent question you'll find it a risky business for you—or any one else!"

The quick blood mounted up to the old mate's forehead, and it looked like as if a fight was coming, but the captain had resumed his supper and the matter ended. But it showed us that he meant to keep to himself.

. . . . .

The *Indiana* made the low-lying atoll at last and lay-to outside. Those on board could see the trader's house close to, but instead of being surrounded by a swarm of eager and excited natives there was not one to be seen. Nor could they even see a canoe coming off. Denison pointed this out to the captain. Although of an evidently savage and morose temperament he was always pleasant enough to Denison in his capacity of supercargo, and inquired of him if he thought the trader had been killed.

"No," Denison said, "I don't think the people here would ever kill Martin; but something is wrong. He has not hoisted his flag, and that is very queer. I can see no natives about his place—which also is curious; and the village just there seems to be deserted. If you will lower the boat I'll soon see what's wrong."

  . . . . .

The skipper called out to lower the whaleboat, put four Rotumah boys in her, and then offered to accompany the supercargo. As he was a new man, Denison naturally was surprised at his wanting to leave his ship at a strange place.

"Glad enough," he said, "the landing here is beastly—lucky if we escape getting stove-in going over the reef. Martin knows the passage well and tackles it in any surf—wish he were here now!"

Captain Chaplin soon took that off his mind. Unconsciously Denison gave him the steer-oar, and in a few minutes they were flying over the reef at a half-tide, and never touched anywhere.

"Why," said Denison, "you seem to know the place."

"I do," he answered, quietly, "know it well, and know Martin, too. You'll find him drunk."

They walked up the white path of broken coral and stood in the doorway of the big front room. At the far end, on a native sofa, lay Martin; by his side sat a young native girl fanning him. No one else.

The gaunt black-whiskered trader tried to rise, but with a varied string of oaths lashed together he fell back, waving his hand to Denison in recognition. The girl was not a native of the island—that could be seen at a glance. She was as handsome as a picture, and after giving the two white men a dignified greeting, in the Yap (Caroline Islands) dialect, she resumed her fanning and smoking her cigarette.

"Martin," said the supercargo, "shake yourself together. What is the matter? Are you sick, or is it only the usual drunk?"

"Both," came in tones that sounded as if his inside were lined with cotton wool; "got a knife in my ribs six months back; never got well; and I've been drinking all the time"—and then, with a silly smile of childish vanity, "all over *her*. She's my new girl—wot d'ye think of her? Ain't she a star?"

. . . . .

All this time Chaplin stood back until Denison called him up and said to the trader, "Our new captain, Martin!"

"By God," said the trader, slowly, "if he ain't the image of that —— nigger-catching skipper that was here from Honolulu four years ago."

"That's me!" said Chaplin, coolly puffing away at his cigar, and taking a seat near the sofa, with one swift glance of admiration at the face of the girl.

In a few minutes Martin told his troubles. Some seven months previously a ship had called at the island. He boarded her. She was a whaler making south to the Kermadecs "sperming." The captain told Martin he had come through the Pelews and picked up a big canoe with a chief's retinue on board, nearly dead from starvation. Many of them did die on board. Among those left were two women, the wife and daughter of the chief—who was the first to die. Making a long story short, Martin gave the captain trade and cash to the tune of five hundred dollars for the two women, and came ashore. Pensioning off his other wife, he took the young girl himself and sold the mother to the local chief for a ton of copra.

A week afterwards a young native came outside his house, cutlass in hand. He was a brother of the dismissed wife and meant fighting. Martin darted out, his new love standing calmly in the doorway, smoking. There was a shot, and the native fell with a bullet through his chest, but raising his voice he called to others and flung them his cutlass; and then Martin found himself struggling with two or three more and got a fearful stab. That night the head men of the village came to him and said that as he had always been a good man to them they would not kill him, but they then and there tabooed him till he either killed his new wife or sent her away. And when he looked out in the morning he saw the whole village going away in canoes to the other side of the lagoon. For six months neither he nor the girl—Lunumala was her name—had spoken to a native. And Martin gave himself up to love and drink, and, since the *fracas*, had not done a cent's worth of trading.

Denison told Martin his instructions. He only nodded, and said something to the girl, who rose and brought the supercargo his books. A few minutes' looking through them, and then at his well-filled trade-room, showed Denison that everything was right, except that all the liquor was gone.

"Martin," the supercargo said, "this won't do. I've got another man aboard, and I'll put him here and take you to Rotumah."

But he swore violently. He couldn't go anywhere else. This island was his home. The natives would give in some day. He'd rather cut his throat than leave.

"Well," said Denison, calmly, "it's one of two

things. You know as well as I do that a *tabu* like this is a serious business. I know you are the best man for the place; but, if you won't leave, why not send the girl away?"

No, he wouldn't send her away. She should stay too.

"All serene," said the man of business. "Then I'll take stock at once, and we'll square up and I'll land the other man."

This was a crusher for poor Martin. Denison felt sorry for him, and had a hard duty to carry through.

Presently the sick man with a ten-ton oath groaned, "—— you, Mister Skipper, wot are you a-doin' of there, squeezin' my wife's hand?"

. . . . .

"Well, now," said the captain, quietly, "look here, Martin. Just put this in your thick head and think it out in five minutes. You've either got to give up this girl or get away from the island. Now, I don't want to make any man feel mean, but she don't particularly care about you, and——"

The graceful creature nodded her approval or Chaplin's remarks, and Martin glared at her. Then he took a drink of gin and meditated.

Two minutes passed. Then Martin turned.

"How much?" he said.

"Fifty pounds, sonny. Two hundred and fifty dollars."

"Easy to see you've been in the business," mumbled Martin; "why, her mother's worth that. 'Tain't no deal."

"Well, then, how much *do* you want?"

"A hundred."

"Haven't got it on board, sonny. Take eighty sovereigns and the rest in trade or liquor?"

"It's a deal," said Martin; "are you game to part ten sovereigns for the girl's mother, and I'll get her back from the natives!"

"No," said Chaplin, rising; "the girl's enough for me."

She had risen and was looking at Martin with a pallid face and set teeth, and then without a word of farewell on either side she picked up a Panama hat and, fan in hand, walked down to the boat and got in, waiting for Chaplin.

. . . . .

Presently he came down, and said, "Well, Mr. Denison, I suppose, as matters are arranged, you'll want to land Martin some trade?"

"Oh, no," said Denison, "he's got plenty. This *tabu* on his own business will teach him a lesson. But I want to send him some provisions on shore. By the way, captain, that girl's likely to prove expensive to you. I hope you'll put her ashore at Rotumah till the voyage is nearly over."

"No," said he, "I won't. Of course, I know our godly owners would raise a deuce of a row about my buying the girl if I couldn't pay for her keep while she's on board, but I've got a couple of hundred pounds in Auckland, as they know, besides some cash on board. After I've paid that thundering lackguard I've still some left, and I mean to put her ashore at Levuka to live until I can take her to her destination."

"Why," Denison queried, "what are you going to do with her?"

"Just this: there's a friend of mine in Honolulu

always willing to give a few thousand dollars for a really handsome girl. And I believe that girl will bring me nearly about three thousand dollars."

. . . . .

For three months the girl remained on board, grave, dignified, and always self-possessed. Chaplin treated her kindly, and it was evident to all on board that the girl had given him such affection as she was capable of, and little knew his intentions regarding her future. With both Chaplin and Denison she would now converse freely in the Pelew Island dialect. And often pointing to the sinking sun she would sigh—" There is my land over there behind the sun. When will we get there?" Laying her hand on Chaplin's she would seek for an answer. And he would answer—nothing.

. . . . .

After the *Indiana* had cruised through the Line Islands she headed back for Rotumah and Fiji. The girl came up on deck after supper. It was blowing freshly and the barque was slipping through the water fast. Lunumala walked to the binnacle and looked at the compass, pointing to S.S.W. She gazed steadily at it awhile and then said to the Rotumah boy in his own tongue—" Why is the ship going to the South?"

Tom, the Rotuman, grinned—" To Fiji, my white tropic bird."

Just then Chaplin came on deck, cigar in mouth. The girl and he looked at each other. He knew by her white, set face that mischief was brewing.

Pointing, with her left hand, to the compass, she said, in a low voice—

" To Fiji?"

A Dead Loss.

"Yes," said Chaplin, coolly, "to Fiji, where you must remain awhile, Lunumala."

"And you?"

"That is my business. Question me no more now. Go below and turn in."

Standing there before him, she looked again in his hard, unrelenting face. Then she slowly walked forward.

"Sulky," said Chaplin to Denison.

Steadily she walked along the deck, and then mounted to the to'gallant fo'c's'le and stood a second or two by the cathead. Her white dress flapped and clung to her slender figure as she turned and looked aft at us, and her long, black hair streamed out like a pall of death. Suddenly she sprang over.

With a curse Chaplin rushed to the wheel, and in double-quick time the whaleboat was lowered and search was made. In half an hour Chaplin returned, and gaining the deck said, in his usual cool way, to the mate: "Hoist in the boat and fill away again as quick as possible." Then he went below.

A few minutes afterwards he was at his accustomed amusement, making tortoise-shell ornaments with a fret-saw.

"A sad end to the poor girl's life," said the supercargo.

"Yes," said the methodical ex-Honolulu blackbirder, "and a sad end to my lovely five hundred dollars."

HICKSON: A HALF-CASTE

Hickson: a Half-Caste.

"Mauki" Hickson and I were coming across from the big native town at Mulinu'u Point to Apia one afternoon when we met a dainty little white woman, garmented in spotless white. Hickson, touching his hat, walked on across the narrow bridge that crosses the creek by the French Mission, and waited for me on the other side.

This tiny lady in white was a lovable little creature. There was not a man in Samoa but felt proud and pleased if she stopped and spoke to him. And she could go anywhere on the beach, from respectable Matautu right down to riotous, dissolute Matafele, and make her purchases at the big store of Der Deutsche Handels Plantagen und Süd See Inseln Gesellschaft without even a drunken native daring to look at her. That was because every one, dissolute native and licentious white, knew she was a good woman. Perhaps, had she been married, and had she had a yellow, tallowy skin and the generally acidulated appearance peculiar to white women long resident in the South Seas, we wouldn't have thought so much of her, and felt mean and contemptible when she taxed us in her open, innocent fashion with doing those things that we ought not have done. But she had a sweet, merry little face, set about with dimples, and soft cheeks hued like the first flush of a ripening peach; and when she spoke to us she brought back memories of other faces like hers—far-away faces that most of us would have liked to have seen again.

. . . . .

Just by the low stone wall, that in those days came close down to the creek, the little lady stood under the shade of some cocoanuts, and spoke to me.

"Who is that horrible, sulky-looking half-caste?" she said, jerking her sunshade towards my late companion.

"That is Hickson, Miss Milly," I said—a very decent, steady fellow, with a white man's heart.

"Decent! steady! and with a white man's heart!" and Miss Milly's pink-and-white cheeks reddened angrily. "How I hate that expression! No wonder all sorts of horrible things happen in these dreadful islands when white men will walk down the road with a cruel, remorseless wretch like Hickson—the man that murdered his sister."

"You should not say that, Miss Milly," I said. "Of course that is the common report, spread about by the captain of the German brig ——. But that is because Hickson nearly killed him for calling him a nigger. And you must remember, Miss Milly, that I was there at the time. Hickson was our second mate. His sister was killed, but it is a cruel thing to accuse him of murdering her; he was very fond of her."

"Oh dear! I am so glad to hear some one say it isn't true," and the bright eyes filled. "They say, too, she was such a pretty little thing. How ever did she get to such a terrible place as Ponape? Come up and see uncle and me before you go away again. Good-bye now, I'm going to buy a water-bag at Goddeffroy's."

. . . .

I think that Hickson must have guessed that he had formed the subject of the conversation between the little lady and myself, for after we had walked on a bit he said, suddenly—

"I think I'll go aboard the *Menchikoff* and ship; she wants some hands, and I would like to clear out of this. Except two or three that have known me for a long time, like yourself, every one looks crooked at me."

"I think you are right, Hickson, in going away. Samoa is a bad place for an idle man. But won't you come another trip with us? The old man[1] thinks a lot of you, and there's always a second mate's berth for you with him."

Hickson's eyes flashed fire. "No! I'd as lief go to hell as ship again with a man that once put me in irons, and disgraced me before a lot of Kanakas. I've got White Blood enough in me to make me remember that. "Good-bye," and he shook hands with me; "I'll wait here till the *Menchikoff's* boat comes ashore and go off and see Bannister."

Poor Hickson. He was proud of his White Blood, and the incident he alluded to was a bitter memory to him. Could he ever forget it? I never could, and thought of it as I was being pulled off on board.

. . . .

It was at Jakoits Harbour—in Ponape—that it

[1] The "old man," *i.e.*, the captain.

happened. Hickson and I were going ashore in the long boat to buy a load of yams for our native crew, when he began to tell me something of his former life.

His had been a strange and chequered career, and in his wanderings as a trader and as a boatsteerer in a Hobart Town whaler, he had traversed every league of the wide Pacific. With his father and two sisters he had, till a few years or so before he joined us, been trading at Yap, in the Western Carolines. Here the wandering old white man had died. Of his two sisters, one, the eldest, had perished with her sailor husband by the capsizing of a schooner which he commanded. The youngest, then about nine years old, was taken care of by the captain of a whaler that touched at Yap, until he placed her in charge of the then newly-founded American Mission at Ponape, and in the same ship Hickson went on his wanderings again, joining us at Tahiti. And I could see as he talked to me that he had a deep affection for her.

"What part of Ponape is she living on?" I asked.

"I don't know, I'm sure. Here, I suppose; and if you don't mind, while you're weighing the yams, I'll go up to the mission-house and inquire."

"Right you are, Hickson," I said, "but don't forget to get back early, it's a beastly risky pull out to the ship in the dark."

We went into a little bay, and found the natives waiting for us with the yams, and Hickson, after inquiring the way to the Mission, left me.

. . . . .

Ponape in those days was a rough place. It was the rendezvous of the American whaling fleet, that came there for wood and water and "other supplies," before they sailed northward along the grim coasts of Japan and Tchantar Bay to the whale grounds of the Arctic Seas.

And sometimes there would be trouble over the "other supplies" among the savagely licentious crews of mixed men of all nations, and knives would flash, and the white sand of the beaches be stuck together in places with patches and clots of dull red. It was the whalers' paradise — a paradise of the loveliest tropical beauty, of palm-shaded beach and verdure-clad mountain imaginable; a paradise of wonderfully beautiful and utterly, hopelessly immoral native women; and, lastly, a paradise of cheap native grog, as potent and fiery as if Hell had been boiled down and concentrated into a small half-pint.

It was dark, and the yams had all been brought and stored in the boat before Hickson returned. By the flickering light of a native fire in a house close by I could see that something was the matter with him. His face was drawn, and his black eyes gleamed out like dully burning coals from the thick wavy hair that fell about his temples.

"I'm sorry I'm late," he said, and the moment he had spoken I knew by the dangerous huskiness of his voice that he had been drinking the native grog.

Staggering into the boat, he sat down beside me and took the tiller.

"Give way, *fanau seoli* (children o hell)," he growled to our crew of Samoans and Rotumah boys, "let us get these yams aboard, and then I'm coming back to burn the —— mission-house down."

Slowly the heavily-laden boat got way on her, and we slid away from the light of the native fire out into the inky blackness of night. Beyond a muttered curse at the crew, and keeping up that horrible grinding of the teeth common enough to men of violent passions when under great excitement, Hickson said nothing further till I asked—

"Hickson, what's the matter? Couldn't you find your sister?"

He sat up straight, and gripping my knee in his left hand till I winced, said, with an awful preliminary burst of blasphemy—

"By God, sir, she's gone to hell; I'll never see poor little Kătia again. I'm not drunk, don't you think it. I did have a stiff pull of grog up in the village there, but I'm not drunk; but there's something running round and round in my head that's drivin' me mad."

"Where is she?" I asked.

"God knows. I went to the mission-house and asked for the white missionary. The —— dog wasn't there. He and his wife are away in Honolulu, on a dollar-cadging trip. There was about three or four of them cursed native teachers in the house, and all I could get out of them was that Kătia wasn't there now; went away a year ago. 'Where to?' I said to one fat pig, with a white shirt and no pants on him. 'Don't know,' says he, in the Ponape lingo; 'she's a bad girl now, and has left us holy ones of God and gone to the whaleships.'"

Coming from any other man but Hickson I could have laughed at this, so truly characteristic of the repellent, canting native missionary of Micronesia, but the quick, gasping breath of Hickson and his trembling hand showed me how he suffered.

"I grabbed him and choked him, till he was near dead, and chucked him in a heap outside. Then I went all round to the other houses, but every one ran away from me. I got a swig of grog from a native house and came right back." Then he was silent, and fixed his eyes on the ship's lights seaward.

I could not offer him any sympathy, so said nothing. Lighting our pipes we gazed out ahead. Far away, nearest the reef, lay our brig, her riding light just discernible. A mile or two further away were three or four American whalers, whose black hulls we could just make out through the darkness. Within five hundred yards of us lay a dismantled and condemned brig, the *Kamehameha IV.*, from whose stern ports came a flood of light and the sounds of women's voices.

We were just about abeam of her when Hickson suddenly exclaimed—

"Why, sir, the boat is sinking. Pull hard, boys, pull for the brig. The water's coming in wholesale over the gunwale. Hadn't you fellows enough sense to leave a place to bale from?" and he slewed the boat's head for the brig.

She had two boats astern. We were just in time to get alongside one and pitch about two tons of yams into her, or we would have sunk.

The noise we made was heard on the brig, and a head was put out of one of the ports, and a voice hailed us. This was the brig's owner and captain, W——.

"Come on board and have a cigar!" he called out.

. . . . . .

Leaving the crew to bale out and re-ship the yams, we clambered on deck.

Now, this brig and her captain had a curious history. She was, two years before, as well-found a whaleship as ever sailed the Pacific, but by some extraordinary ill-luck she had never taken a fish during a cruise of seven months, although in the company of others that were doing well. The master, one of those fanatically religious New Englanders that by some strange irony of fate may be often met with commanding vilely licentious crews of whaleships, was a skilled and hitherto lucky man. On reaching Ponape the whole of his officers and crew deserted *en masse,* and went off in other ships. Utterly helpless, W—— was left by himself. There were, of course, plenty of men to be had in Ponape, but the ship's reputation for bad luck damned his hopes of getting a fresh crew.

Whether the man's brain was affected by his troubles I know not, but after living like a hermit for a year, alone on the brig, a sudden change took place in his character and conduct. Sculling ashore in one of his boats—she was a four-boat ship—he had an interview with Nanakin, the chief of the Jakoit's district, and returned on board with five or six young girls, to whom he gave permanent quarters on board, selling from time to time his sails, whaling gear, and trade to keep his harem in luxury. At the end of a year the brig was pretty well stripped of all of any value; and W—— went utterly, hopelessly mad.

. . . . .

The brig's cabin was large and roomy. The table

that had once nearly filled it had been taken away, and the floor covered with those peculiarly made Ponape mats which, by rolling up one-half of either end, forms a combined couch and pillow. As Hickson and I, following the crazy little captain, made our appearance, some four young girls, who were lolling about on the mats, started up, and looked at us with big, wondering eyes, ablaze with curiosity.

Both Hickson and myself—and he had roved throughout Polynesia from his boyhood—were struck by the extraordinary beauty of these four young creatures; so young and innocent in looks; in sin, as old as Ninon d'Enclos.

Placing one hand on the shoulder of the girl nearest to him, and fixing his big, blue, deep-set eyes on us, W—— waved the other towards the girls, and said—

"Welcome, gentlemen, welcome. Behold these little devils, who in the guise of sunburnt angels are the solace of a man forgotten by his God, and the father of a family residing in Martha's Vineyard, United States of America."

Then he gave us each a cigar and told us to be seated while he got us a glass of New England rum.

. . . . .

Hickson, with a contemptuous smile, sat with folded arms on a short, heavy stool. One of the girls, unshipping one of the two lights from the hook on which it hung, followed W—— into a state-room to get the rum. Presently we heard them coming out, W—— carrying a wickerwork-covered five-gallon jar; but two girls came out instead of one. The stranger kept close to W——, one hand holding the sleeve of his shirt.

Stooping as he set the jar on the floor, I had a good view of the new-comer, and a deadly fear seized me. I knew at once that she was Hickson's sister! He was coarse and rough-looking, but yet a handsome man, and this girl's likeness to him was very striking. Just then Hickson, not even noticing her, rose and said he was going on deck to see if the boat was ready, when the strange quavering tones of W—— arrested him.

"Be seated, sir, for another minute. Nijilon, get some glasses. You see here, gentlemen, the fairest and choicest of all my devil-vestals, one that——"

Hickson looked at her, and with a terrified wail the girl clutched W——'s arm, and placed her face against his breast. With lips drawn back from his white teeth the half-caste sprang up, and his two clenched hands pawed the air. Then from his throat there came a sound like a laugh strangled into a groan.

Scarce knowing what I did I got in front of him. He dashed me aside as if I were a child, and seized the stool. And as he swung it round above his head the girl raised a face like the hue of death to his; then the blow fell, and she and W—— went down together.

.   .   .   .   .

Hickson rushed on deck and tried to spring overboard. I think he must have struck the main boom, for one of our crew who was on deck heard him fall. We got a light, and found him lying senseless. Two of the "vestals" held him up while I went below for some rum and water. W——was lying where he had fallen, breathing heavily, but not seriously injured as far as I could see. But one look at the closed eyes of the girl told me she was past all help. The heavy stool had struck her on the temple.

Placing Hickson in the boat with two men to mind him, I took the other two with me into the cabin of the brig. W—— was seated on the floor, held up by two of his harem, and muttering unintelligibly to himself. The other two were bending over the figure on the floor, and placing their hands on her bosom.

"Come away from here, L——," said Harry, one of our Rotumah boys, to me; "if the Ponape men come off, they will kill us all."

We could do nothing, so we got back into the boat, and with the still senseless body of Hickson lying at our feet, pulled out to the ship.

· · · · ·

When he came to he was a madman, and for his own safety our captain put him in irons. We put to sea next day, our skipper, like a wise man, saying it would go hard with us if W—— died, and four Yankee whalers in port.

The day after we got away Hickson was set at liberty, and went about his duties as usual. At nightfall I went into his deck cabin. He was lying in his bunk, in the dark, smoking. He put out his hand, and drew me close up to him.

"Harry says she is dead?"

"Yes," I whispered.

"Poor little Kătia; I never meant to hurt her. But I am glad she is dead."

And he smoked his pipe in silence.

A BOATING PARTY OF TWO

A Boating Party of Two.

THE prison gate opened, and Number 73 for a minute or so leaned against the wall to steady himself. The strange clamour of the streets smote upon his ear like dagger strokes into his heart, and his breath came in quick, short gasps.

Some one was speaking to him—a little, pale-faced, red-whiskered man with watery eyes—and Challoner, once "Number 73," staring stupidly at him, tried to understand, but failed. Then, sidling up to him, the little man took one of Challoner's gaunt and long hands between his own, and a stout, masculine female in a blue dress and poke bonnet and spectacles clasped the other and called him "brother."

A dull gleam shone in his sullen eyes at last, and drawing his hands away from them, he asked—

"Who are you?"

The stout woman's sharp tongue clattered, and Challoner listened stolidly. Sometimes a word or two in the volley she fired would cause him to shake his head wearily—"happiness in the life heternal," "washed in the blood of the Lamb," and "cast yer sins away an' come an' be saved without money an' without price."

Then he remembered who he was and who they were—the warders had told him of the Prison Gate Brigade. He turned to the man and muttered—

"I want to get away from here," and stepped past them, but the woman laid her fat, coarse hand on his sleeve.

"Come 'ome with us, brother. P'r'aps yer 'ave a mother or a wife waitin' to 'ear from yer, an' we——"

He dashed her hand aside savagely—"Blast you, no; let me go!"

Then with awkward, shambling gait he pushed through the curious crowd at the prison gate, crossed the street, and entered the nearest public-house.

"Another soul escaped us, Sister Hannah," squeaked the little man; "but we'll try and rescue him when he comes out from the house of wickedness and abomination."

"Better leave him alone," said a warder in plain clothes, who just then came through the gate, "he won't be saved at no price, I can tell yer."

"Who is the poor man?" asked Sister Hannah, in a plaintive, injured voice.

"Sh! Mustn't ask them questions," said the little man.

But he knew, all the same, that the tall, gaunt man with the sallow face and close-cropped white hair was Harvey Challoner, once chief officer of the ship *Victory*, sentenced in Melbourne to imprisonment for life for manslaughter, but released at the end of ten years.

. . . . .

The *Victory* murder trial had not attracted much public attention, and the prisoner had been defended

A Boating Party of Two.

at the public expense. On the voyage from London to Australia the crew had become discontented. They had reason for their discontent. Captain Cressingham, for all his suave, gentlemanly shore manners, was an adept at "hazing," and was proud of the distinction of making every ship he commanded a hell to the fo'c's'le hands. Sometimes, with sneering, mocking tongue, he would compliment Challoner upon the courteous manner in which he "addressed the gentlemen for'ard." As for the other two mates, they were equally as brutal as their captain, but lacked his savage, methodical vindictiveness.

When only a few weeks out, Harman, the second mate, one day accused one of the men of "soldiering," and striking him in the face, broke his nose, and as the man lay on the deck he kicked him brutally. Challoner, who was on deck at the time, jumped down off the poop, and seizing Harman by the arm, called him a cowardly hound.

"And you're a d——d old woman," was the retort.

Challoner's passion overpowered him, and at the end of five minutes Harman was carried below badly knocked about, and a stormy scene ensued between Challoner and the captain.

"You have all but killed Mr. Harman. I could, and should, put you in irons for the rest of the voyage," the captain had said.

There was a steely glitter in the mate's dark eyes as he answered—

"In dealing with ruffians such as Harman and yourself one doesn't stop at an extra blow or two."

From that time Cressingham was his bitter enemy; but Challoner did his duty as chief officer too faithfully to give the captain a chance against him.

Day after day had passed. The sullen discontent of the crew had changed into outspoken hatred and a thirst for revenge upon the captain and Harman and Barton—the latter the third mate—and Challoner, who knew what was brewing, dared not open his mouth to any one of the three upon the subject. Between himself and Cressingham and the other two there had now sprung up a silent yet fierce antagonism, which the crew were quick to perceive, and from which they augured favourably for themselves.

One night, just as Challoner had relieved the second mate, some of the hands from both watches marched boldly aft and asked him if he would take command of the ship. He had only to say the word, they said. They were tired of being "bashed" and starved to death by the skipper and two mates, and if he would navigate the ship to Melbourne they would keep him free from interference, and take the consequences, &c.

"Go for'ard, you fools," said Challoner, with assumed harshness, "don't talk mutiny to me."

A step sounded on the deck behind him, and Cressingham's sneering tones were heard.

"Discussing mutiny, are you, Mr. Challoner? By God, sir, I've suspected you long enough. Go below, sir; or go for'ard with these fellows. You'll do no more mate's duty aboard of this ship. Ah, Colliss, you're one of the ringleaders, are you?" And in an instant he seized a seaman by the throat, and called loudly for Barton and Harman to help him.

Before they could respond to his call the poop was

black with struggling men. Cressingham, mad with passion, had Colliss down trying to strangle him, and Challoner, fearing murder would be done, had thrown himself upon the captain and tried to make him release his grip of the man's throat. At that moment a sailor called out—

"Stand by, chaps, for Barton and Harman, and drop 'em the moment they shows up. Mr. Challoner's got the old man safe."

But Messrs. Harman and Barton were tough customers. The loud cries on deck and heavy tramping of feet told them that a crisis had occurred, and they dashed up, each with a revolver in hand—only to be felled from behind ere they could fire a shot. Challoner, letting the captain free, sprang to their aid. But he came too late, for before, with blows, kicks, and curses, he could force his way through the swaying, surging mass of men that hid the fallen officers from his view, he heard a sound—the sound of a man's skull as it was smashed in by a heavy blow.

"He's done for," said a voice, with a savage laugh, "scoot, chaps, scoot. This shindy will keep the old man quiet a bit, now one of his fightin' cocks is gone," and the men tumbled down off the poop as quick as their legs could carry them, leaving Challoner and the two prone figures behind them. Cressingham had gone below for his revolver.

"Steward," called Challoner, "bring a light here, quick, and see where the captain is," and, stooping down, he tried to raise Harman, then laid him down with a shudder—his brains were scattered on the deck. Barton was alive, but unconscious.

As Challoner was about to rise, Captain Cressingham stood over him and raised his arm, and dealt him a crashing blow with a belaying pin. When he regained consciousness he was in irons.

. . . . .

A month later and he stood in the dock charged with murder. The principal witnesses against him were his captain and Barton, the third mate. The crew, who, of course, were also witnesses in the case, didn't worry much about him. It wasn't likely they would run their necks into a noose if it could be placed round any one else's. And in this instance—superinduced by a vision of the gallows—fo'c's'le hands stuck to one another and lied manfully together. None of them "had hurt Mr. Harman."

But it was upon Cressingham's evidence that his fate hung; and Cressingham, suave, handsome, and well-dressed, told the court how Challoner had once attempted to murder Harman in the earlier part of the voyage. Barton, with his arm in a sling, corroborated the lie with blunt cheerfulness.

His Honour summed up dead against the prisoner, and the jury, impressed by the calm, gentlemanly appearance of Captain Cressingham, and the haggard, unshaven, and guilty look of the man whose life they held in their hands, were not long in considering their verdict.

The prisoner was found guilty, but with a recommendation to mercy.

And then the judge, who was cross and tired, made a brief but affecting speech, and sentenced him to imprisonment for life.

He went into his prison cell with hair as black as

night, and came out again as white as a man of seventy.

* * * * *

In a back room of the public-house he sat and waited till he had courage and strength enough to face the streets again. And as he waited, he gave himself up to visions of the future—to the day when, with his hand on Cressingham's lying throat, he would see his face blacken and hear the rattling agonies of his gasps for breath. He leaned back in his chair and laughed hoarsely. The unearthly, hideous sound startled him, and he glanced round nervously as if he feared to betray his secret. Then he drank another glass of brandy, and with twenty-six shillings of prison money in his pocket and ten years of the blackest hatred in his heart, he went out again into the world to begin his search—for Cressingham and revenge.

II.

The people of Port ——, on the east coast of New Zealand, were charmed with the handsome commander of the biggest ocean steamer that had yet visited the port, and on the eve of his departure gave Captain Cressingham the usual banquet. Banquets to captains of new lines of steamers are good things to boom the interests of a budding seaport town, and so a few score of the "warmest" men in the place cheerfully planked down their guinea each for the occasion.

The *Belted Will* had hauled out from the wharf and lay a mile or so from the shore ready for sea, and the captain had told his chief officer to send a boat ashore for him at twelve o'clock.

Among the crowd that lounged about the entrance to the town hall and watched for the arrival of the guest of the evening was a tall, dark, rough-looking man with white curly hair. One or two of those present seemed to know him, and presently some one addressed him.

"Hallo, Harry! come to have a look at the swells? 'Taint often you come out o' nights."

The white-haired man nodded without speaking, and then moved away again. Presently the man he was looking for was driven up, and the loungers drew aside to let him pass up the steps into the blaze of light under the vestibule of the hall, where he was welcomed by half a dozen effusive citizens. For a moment he stood and chatted, and the man who watched clenched his brawny hands and ground his teeth. Then Captain Cressingham disappeared, and the tall man walked slowly away again in the direction of the wharves.

. . . . .

At eleven o'clock Cressingham's boat came ashore, and the crew as they made her fast grumbled and cursed in true sailor fashion.

"Are you the chaps from the *Belted Will?*" said a man, who was leaning against one of the wharf sheds.

"Yes; who are you, mister?" said one of them.

"I'm Harry—one of the hands that was stowing wool aboard. I heard you was coming ashore for the captain, and as you won't see him for the next couple of hours, I thought I'd come down and ask you to come up and have a couple of nips. It's cold loafing about here. I live pretty close."

"You're one o' the right sort. What say, Peter?"

Peter was only too glad. The prospect of getting into a warm house was enough inducement, even without the further bliss of a couple of nips.

In half an hour the two men were helplessly drunk in Harry's room, and their generous host carefully placing another bottle (not doctored this time) of rum on the table for them when they awoke, quietly went out and locked the door behind him. Then he walked quickly back to where the *Belted Will's* boat lay, and descending the steps, got into her and seemed to busy himself for a while. He soon found what he was looking for, and then came the sound of inrushing water. Then he drew the boat up again to the steps, got out, and casting off the painter, slung it aboard, and shoved her into the darkness.

. . . . .

For another hour he waited patiently, and then came the rattle of wheels, and loud voices and laughter, as a vehicle drew up at the deserted wharf.

"Why not stay ashore to-night, captain," said one of the guest's champagne-laden companions, "and tell your man to go back?"

"No, no," laughed Cressingham. "I don't like the look of the weather, and must get aboard right away. Boat ahoy! Where are you, men?"

"Your boat isn't here, sir," said a gruff voice, and a tall man advanced from the darkness of the sheds. "I saw the men up town, both pretty full, and heard them laughing and say they meant to have a night ashore. It's my belief they turned her adrift purposely."

Cressingham cursed them savagely, and then turned to the tall man.

"Can you get me a boat?"

"Well, sir, there's a big heavy boat belonging to my boss that I can get, and I don't mind putting you aboard. We can sail out with this breeze in no time. She's lying under the coal-wharf."

"That'll do. Good-bye, gentlemen. I trust we shall all meet again in another eight months or so."

The big man led the way, and in a few minutes they reached the coal wharf, under which the boat was moored. She was a heavy, clumsily-built craft, and Cressingham, on getting aboard and striking a match, cursed her filthy state. The tall man stepped to the mast and hoisted the lug-sail, and Cressingham, taking the tiller, kept her out towards the *Belted Will,* whose riding light was discernible right ahead.

"We must look out for the buoys, sir," said the gruff-voiced man, as the breeze freshened up and the heavy boat quickened her speed.

"All right," said Cressingham, and pulling out a cigar from his overcoat he bent his head and struck a light.

Ere he raised it the white-haired man had sprung upon him like a tiger, and seized his throat in his brawny hands. For a minute or so Cressingham struggled in that deadly grip, and then lay limp and insensible in the bottom of the boat.

Challoner, with malignant joy, leaned over him with a world of hate in his black eyes, and then proceeded to business.

Lifting the unconscious man he carried him for'ard, and, placing him upon a thwart, gagged and bound him securely. Then he went aft and, taking the tiller, hauled the sheet in and kept the boat away again upon her course for the *Belted Will.*

He passed within a quarter of a mile of the huge, black mass with the bright riding light shining upon the fore-stay, and the look-out from the steamer took no notice of the boat as she swept past toward the open sea.

· · · · ·

Daylight at last. For six hours the boat had swept before the strong northerly wind, and the land lay nearly thirty miles astern, lost in a sombre bank of heavy clouds and mist. Challoner had taken off his rough overcoat and thrown it over the figure of his enemy. He did not want him to perish of cold. And as he steered he fixed his eyes, lighted up with an unholy joy, upon the bent and crushed figure before him.

Cressingham was conscious now, and stared with horror-filled eyes at the grim creature in the craft before him—a gaunt, dark-faced man, clad in a striped guernsey and thin cotton pants, with a worn and ragged woollen cap stuck upon his thick masses of white curly hair. Who was he? A madman.

Challoner seemed to take no notice of him, and looked out upon the threatening aspect of sea and sky with an unconcerned face. Presently he hauled aft the sheet a bit, and kept the boat on a more westerly course, and the bound and wondering man on the for'ard thwart watched his movements intently.

The boat had made a little water, and the white-headed man stooped and baled it out carefully; then he looked up and caught his prisoner's eye.

"Ha, ha, Cressingham, how are you? Isn't it delightful that we should meet again?"

A strange inarticulate cry broke from Cressingham.

"Who are you?"

"What! is it possible that you don't remember me? I am afraid that that banquet champagne has affected you a little. Try back, my dear fellow. Don't you remember the *Victory?*"

Ah! he remembered now, and a terrible fear chilled his life-blood and froze his once sneering tongue into silence.

"Ah! I see you do," and Challoner laughed with Satanic passion. "And so we meet again—with our positions reversed. Once, unless my memory fails me, you put me in irons. Now, Captain Cressingham, I have you seized up, and we can have a quiet little chat—all to ourselves."

No answer came from Cressingham. With dilated, horror-stricken eyes and panting breath he was turned into stone. The wretched man's silence at last broke up the depths of his maddened tormentor's hatred, and with a bound he sprang to his feet and raised his hand on high.

"Ah! God is good to me at last, Cressingham. For ten years I hungered and thirsted for the day that would set me free, free to search the world over for the lying, murderous dog that consigned me, an innocent man, to a lifelong death. And when the day came, sooner than I thought or you thought—for I suffered for ten years instead of for life—I waited, a free man till I got you into my power."

His hand fell to his side again, and then he leaned forward and laughed.

Cressingham, with death creeping into his heart, at last found his voice.

"Are you going to murder me?" he said.

"Yes," said Challoner, slowly, "I am going to murder you. But not quickly. There would be no joy in that. I want you to taste some of my hideous past—some little space, if only for a day or two, of that ten long years of agony I spent in Pentridge."

Then he sat down again, and opening the locker in the stern sheets, took out food and water, and placing it beside him, ate and drank. But he gave none to Cressingham.

He finished his meal, and then looked again at his prisoner, and spoke calmly again.

"You are comfortable, I trust, Captain Cressingham? Not cold, I am certain, for you have my overcoat in addition to your own. Do you know why I gave it to you? Just to keep you nice and warm during the night, and—alive. But, as I feel chilly myself now, I'll take it from you. Thanks," and he laughed mockingly as he leaned over and snatched it away.

"You see, sir, we are going on a long cruise—down to the Snares, perhaps—and I must keep warm myself, or else how can I talk to you to break the monotony of the voyage? . . . It is no use looking astern, my friend. There's only one tug in port, and she is not in sea-going trim, so we've got a good start of any search party. And as I don't want to die myself, we won't run away from the land altogether."

And so the day passed, agony and deadly fear

blanching the face of one, and cruel, murderous joy filling the heart of the other. Once, as the last dying gleams of the wintry sun for a few brief moments shone over the blackened waters, Challoner saw a long stream of steamer's smoke between the boat and the misty line of coast, and he lowered the sail and let the boat drift till darkness enwrapped them again.

Once more he took out food and water, and ate and drank, and then lit his pipe and smoked, and watched with eyes that glared with the lust of murder and revenge the motionless being before him.

Only once in all that night of horror to Cressingham did he speak, and his voice shook and quivered, and came in choking gasps.

"Challoner, for the love of Christ, kill me and end my misery."

"Ha! still alive, Captain Cressingham! That is very satisfactory—to me only, of course. Kill you, did you say?" and again his wild demoniac laugh pealed out through the black loneliness of the night. "No, I don't intend to kill you. I want to see you suffer and die by inches. I want you to call upon God to help you, so that I can mock at you, and defy Him to rob me of my vengeance."

A shuddering moan, and then silence again.

Again the day broke, and as the ocean mists cleared and rolled away, and the grey morning light fell upon the chilled and stiffening form of his enemy, Challoner came up and looked into his face, and spoke to him.

No answer came from his pallid lips, and Challoner thrust his hand under Cressingham's coat and felt his heart. He was still alive, and presently the closed and swollen eyelids opened, and as he met the glance of the man who leaned over him an anguished groan burst from his heart.

Challoner looked at him intently for awhile; then he hoisted the sail again, and, taking the tiller, headed the boat in for the land. The wind had hauled round during the night, and although the boat made a lot of leeway there was no danger now of being blown away from the land altogether.

As the sun mounted higher, and the grey outlines of the shores darkened, he glanced carefully over the sea to the north-west. Nothing in sight there. But as the boat lifted to a sea he saw about five miles to leeward that a big steamer was coming up. In half an hour, unless she changed her course, she would be up to the boat and could not fail to see her.

In five minutes more Cressingham lay in the bottom of the boat unbound, but dying fast, and Challoner was speaking to him.

"Cressingham, you are dying. You know that, don't you? And you know that I am not lying when I tell you that there is a steamer within five miles of us. In less than half an hour she will be up to us."

One black, swollen hand was raised feebly, and then fell back, and a hoarse sound came from his throat.

"Well, now listen. I said I wanted to see you die—die as you are dying now—with my face over yours, watching you die. And you die and I live. I can live now, Cressingham, and perhaps the memory of those ten years of death in life that I suffered through you will be easier to bear. And yet there is one thing more that you must know—something that will make it harder for you to meet your Maker, but easier for me. . . . Listen." He knelt beside him and almost shrieked it: "I had no one in the whole world to care for me when I was tried for my life but my wife—and you, you fiend, you murderer—you killed her. She died six years ago—starved and died.

Cressingham, with closed eyes, lay with his head supported on Challoner's left arm. Presently a tremor shook his frame, a fleck of foam bubbled from between his lips, and then the end.

With cold, merciless eyes the other regarded him, with clenched hands and set teeth. Then he went for'ard and unbent the boat's kedge, and with the same lashings that had bound the living man to the thwart he lashed the kedge across the dead man's chest.

He stood up and looked at the approaching steamer, and then he raised the body in his arms and dropped it over the side.

. . . . .

A few days later the papers said that the steamer *Maungatapu* had picked up a man named Harry, who with Captain Cressingham, of the *Belted Will*, had been blown out to sea from Port ——. It appeared from the survivor's statement that during a heavy squall the same night Captain Cressingham had fallen overboard, and his companion was unable to rescue him.

"THE BEST ASSET IN A FOOL'S ESTATE"

11

"*The Best Asset in a Fool's Estate.*"

A SLIGHT smile lit up the clear-cut, sombre face of Lawson from Safune, as looking up from his boat at Etheridge's house he saw the glint of many lights shining through the walls of the roughly-built store. It was well on towards midnight when he had left Safune and sailed round to Etheridge's, a distance of twelve or fifteen miles, and as his boat touched the sand the first streaks of dawn were changing the dead whiteness of the beach into a dull grey—soon to brighten into a creamy yellow as the sun pierced the heavy land-mist.

A native or two, wrapped from head to foot in the long *lava lava* of white calico, passed him as he followed the windings of the track to Etheridge's, but gave him no sign of greeting. Had he been any one of the few other white men living on Savaii the dark men would have stopped him and, native-like, inquired the reason of his early visit to their town. But they knew Lawson too well. *Matāaitu* they called him—devil-faced. And in this they were not far wrong, for Lawson, with his dark olive skin, jet black beard, and eyes that belied the ever-smiling lips, was not a man whom people would be unanimous in trusting.

The natives knew him better than did his few white acquaintances in Samoa, for here, among them, the mask that hid his inner nature from his compeers was sometimes put aside, though never thrown away. But Etheridge, the hot-blooded young Englishman and friend of six months' standing, thought and spoke of him as "the best fellow in the world."

. . . . .

Etheridge had been taking stock, and the wearisome work had paled his usually florid features. His face flushed with pleasure at Lawson's quiet voice:—

"Hard at it, Etheridge? I don't know which looks the paler—you or Lália. Why on earth didn't you send for me sooner? Any one would think you were some poor devil of a fellow trading for the Dutchmen instead of being an independent man. Now, I'm hungry and want breakfast—that is, if Lália isn't too tired to get it," and he looked compassionately at Etheridge's young half-caste wife, sister to his own.

"I'm not tired," said the girl, quietly. "I've had easy tasks—counting packets of fish-hooks, grosses of cotton, and things like that. Billy wouldn't let me help him with the prints and heavy things," and with the faintest shadow of a smile on her lips she passed through into the sitting-room and thence outside to the little thatched cook-house a few yards away. With ardent infatuation Etheridge rested his blue eyes on the white-robed, slender figure as she stood at the door and watched the Niuĕ cook light his fire for an early cup of coffee—the first overture to breakfast at Etheridge's.

. . . . .

"By Jove, Lawson, I'm the luckiest man in Samoa to get such a wife as Lália—and I only a new-chum to the Islands. I believe she'd work night and day if I'd allow it. And if it hadn't been for you I'd never have met her at all, but would have married some fast creature who'd have gone through me in a month and left me a dead-broken beachcomber."

"Yes," said Lawson, "she *is* a good girl, and, except her sister, about the only half-caste I ever knew whom I would trust implicitly. Their mother was a Hervey Island woman, as I told you, and Lália has been with Terere and me all over Polynesia, and I think I know her nature. She's fond of you, Etheridge, in her quiet, undemonstrative way, but she's a bit shy yet. You see, you don't speak either Rarotongan or Samoan, and half-caste wives hate talking English. Now, tell me, what is it worrying you? You haven't had another attack?"

"Yes," said the younger man, "I have—and a bad one, too, and that's why I sent for you. The stock-taking is nothing; but I was afraid I might get another that would stiffen me properly. Look here, Lawson, you've been a true friend to me. You picked me up six months ago a drunken, half-maddened beast in Apia and saved my life, reason, and money, and——"

"Bosh!" said Lawson, taking his coffee from the hand of Etheridge's wife; "don't think of it, my boy. Every man goes a bit crooked sometimes; so don't thank me too much."

Etheridge waited till his wife was gone and then resumed: "I've been horribly scared, Lawson, over this," and he placed his hand over his heart, "I was lifting a case of biscuits when I dropped like a pithed bullock. When I came to, Lália was bathing my face. . . . I feel pretty shaky still. The doctor at Goddeffroy's warned me, too—said I'd go off suddenly if I wasn't careful. My father and one brother died like that. And I want to talk things over with you in case, you know."

Lawson nodded.

"Everything I have is for her, Lawson—land, house, trade, and money. You're pretty sure there's no irregularity in that will of mine, aren't you?"

"Sure. It's very simply written. It's properly witnessed, and would hold in any court of law if contested. And perhaps your people in Australia might do that."

Etheridge reddened. "No; I cut adrift from 'em long ago. Grog, you know. Beyond yourself and Lália, I haven't a soul who'll bother about me. I think, Lawson, I'll take a run up to Apia and see the Dutch doctor again. Fearful cur, am I not?"

"Come, Etheridge," and Lawson laid his smooth, shapely hand—how dishonest are shapely hands!—on the other's arm. "You're a little down. Anything wrong with one's heart always gives a man a bad shaking. There's Lália calling us to breakfast, so I won't say any more but this: Even if Lália wasn't my wife's sister, and anything happened to you, there's always a home for her in my house. I'd do that for your sake alone, old man, putting aside the principle I go on of showing respect to any white man's wife, even if she were a Oahu girl and had rickety ideas of morality."

· · · · ·

When Lawson had first met him and had carried him down to his station on Savaii, nursed him through his illness, and treated him like a brother, Etheridge, with the impulsive confidence of his simple nature, poured out his thanks and told his history, and eagerly accepted Lawson's suggestion to try his hand at trading, instead of continuing his erratic wanderings—wanderings which could only end in his "going broke" at Tahiti or Honolulu. Fifteen miles or so away, Lawson said, there was a village with a good opening for a trader. How much could he put into it? Well, he had £500 with him, and there was another thousand in Sydney—the last of five. Ample, said his host. So one day the land was bought, a house and store put up, and Etheridge commenced life as a trader.

The strange tropic beauty of the place and the ways of the people soon cast their spell over Etheridge's imaginative nature, and he was as happy as a man possibly could be—with a knowledge that his life hung by a thread. How slender that thread was Lawson knew, perhaps, better than he. The German doctor had said, "You must dell him to be gareful, Mr. Lawson. Any excidemend, any zooden drouble mit anydings; or too much visky midout any excidemends, and he drop dead. I dell you."

.   .   .   .   .

A month or so after he had settled, Etheridge paid his weekly visit to Lawson, and met Lália.

"This is my wife's sister," said Lawson; "she has been on a visit to some friends in Tutuila, and came back in the *Iserbrook*."

The clear-cut, refined, and beautiful features of the

girl did their work all too quickly on Etheridge. He was not a sensualist, only a man keenly susceptible to female beauty, and this girl was beautiful—perhaps not so beautiful as her sister, Terere, Lawson's wife, but with a softer and more tender light in her full, dark eyes. And Lawson smiled to himself when Etheridge asked him to come outside and smoke when his wife and her sister had said good-night. A student of human nature, he had long ago read the simple mind of Etheridge as he would an open book, and knew what was coming. They went outside and talked— that is, Etheridge did. Lawson listened and smoked. Then he put a question to the other man.

. . . . .

"Of course I will, Lawson; do you think I'm scoundrel enough to dream of anything else? We'll go up to Apia and get married by the white missionary."

Lawson laughed in his quiet way. "I wouldn't think you a scoundrel at all, Etheridge. I may as well tell you that I'm not married to her sister. We neglected doing that when I lived in the eastward groups, and no one in Samoa is any the wiser, and wouldn't think anything of it if they were. But although I'm only a poor devil of a trader, I'm a man of principle in some things. Lália is but a child, so to speak, and I'm her natural protector. Now, you're a fellow of some means, and if anything did happen to you she wouldn't get a dollar if she wasn't legally your wife. The consul would claim everything until he heard from your relatives. And she's very young, Etheridge, and you've told me often enough that your heart's pretty dicky. Don't think me a brute."

"The Best Asset in a Fool's Estate." 153

Etheridge grasped his hand and wrung it. "No, no—a thousand times no. You're the best-hearted fellow in the world, and I honour you all the more, Lawson. Will you ask her to-morrow?"

Perhaps if he had heard the manner of Lawson's asking it would have puzzled his simple brain. And the subdued merriment of the two sisters might have caused him to wonder still more.

A week or so after, Etheridge and the two sisters went up to Apia. Lawson was unable to go. Copra was coming in freely, he had said with a smile, and he was too poor to run away from business—even to the wedding of his own wife's sister.

. . . . .

As Etheridge and his young wife came out of the mission church some natives and white loafers stood around and watched them.

"Ho, Māgalo," said one, "is not that *teine*, the sister of the wife of *Matāaitu*, the black-visaged *papalagi*?"

"Aye," answered a skinny old hag, carrying a basket of water-bottles, "'tis she, and the other is Terere. I lived with them once at Tutuila. She who is now made a wife and looketh so good and holy went away but a year ago with the captain of a ship—a pig of a German—and now, look you, she marrieth an Englishman."

The other natives laughed, and then an ugly fat-faced girl with lime-covered head and painted cheeks called out "Pāpatetele!" and Terere turned round and cursed them in good English.

"What does that mean?" said a white man to Flash Harry from Saleimoa—a man full of island lore.

"Why, it means as the bride isn't all as she purfesses to be. Them pretty soft-lookin' ones like her seldom is, in Samoa or anywhere else."

· · · · ·

The day following the stock-taking Etheridge went to Apia—and never came back.

One night a native tapped gently at Lawson's window and handed him a note. As he read Terere with a sleepy yawn awoke, and, stretching one rounded arm out at full length, let it fall lazily on the mat-bed.

"What is it, Harry?"

"Get up, d—— you! Etheridge is dead, and I'm going to take Lália up to Apia as quick as I can. Why the h—— couldn't he die here?"

A rapid vision of unlimited presents from the rich young widow passed through the mind of Terere—to whom the relations that had formerly existed between her and Lawson were well known—as she and he sped along in his boat to Etheridge's. Lália received the news with much equanimity and a few tears, and then leaving Terere in charge, she got into the boat and rolled a cigarette. Lawson was in feverish haste. He was afraid the consul would be down and baulk his rapid but carefully arranged scheme. At Safune he sent his crew of two men ashore to his house for a breaker of water, and then once they were out of sight he pushed off and left them. They were in the way and might spoil everything. The breeze was strong, and that night Lawson and Lália, instead of being out in the open sea beating up to Apia, were ashore in the sitting-room of the white missionary house on the other side of Savaii.

· · · · ·

"I am indeed glad to make your acquaintance, Mr. Lawson. Your honourable impulse deserves commendation. I have always regretted the fact that a man like you whose reputation as an educated and intelligent person far above that of most traders here is not unknown to me"—Lawson smiled sweetly—"should not alone set at defiance the teaching of Holy Writ, but tacitly mock at *our* efforts to inculcate a higher code of morality in these beautiful islands. Ere long I trust I may make the acquaintance of your brother-in-law, Mr. Etheridge, and his wife."

Lawson smiled affably, and a slight tinge suffused the creamy cheek of Lália.

"And now, Mr. Lawson, as you are so very anxious to get back home I will not delay. Here are my wife and my native assistant as witnesses. Stand up, please."

. . . . .

"Get in, you little beast," said Lawson, as he bundled Lália into the boat and started back home, "and don't fall overboard. I don't want to lose the Best Asset in that Fool's Estate."

. . . . .

When the consul, a week later, came down to take possession of Etheridge's "estate," he called in at Safune to ask Lawson to come and help him to take an inventory. Terere met him with a languid smile, and, too lazy perhaps to speak English, answered his questions in Samoan.

"He's married and gone," she said.

"Married? Aren't *you* Mrs. Lawson?" said the bewildered consul, in English.

"Not now, sir; my sister is. Will you take me to Apia in your boat, please?"

. . . . .

And that is how Lawson, the *papalagi mativa* (poor white) and "the best-hearted fellow in the world," became a *mau aloa*—a man of riches, and went, with the Best Asset in Etheridge's estate, the calm-eyed Lália, to start a hotel in—well, no matter where.

DESCHARD OF ONEAKA

Deschard of Oneaka.

I.

AMONG the Gilbert Group—that chain of low-lying sandy atolls annexed by the British Government two years ago—there is one island that may be said to be both fertile and beautiful; yet for all this Kuria—for so it is called by the natives of the group generally—has remained almost uninhabited for the past forty years. Together with the lagoon island of Aranuka, from which it is distant about six miles, it belongs to the present King of Apamama, a large and densely populated atoll situated half a degree to the eastward. Thirty years ago, however, the grandfather of the lad who is now the nominal ruler of Apamama had cause to quarrel with the Kurians, and settled the dispute by invading their island and utterly destroying them, root and branch. To-day it is tenanted only by the young king's slaves.

Of all the many groups and archipelagoes that stud the North and South Pacific from the rocky, jungle-covered Bonins to Juan Fernandez, the islands of the Gilbert Group are—save for this Kuria—the most uninviting and monotonous in appearance. They are for the most part but narrow strips of sandy soil, densely clothed, it is true, with countless thousands of stately cocoanut palms varied with groves of pandanus and occasional patches of stunted scrub, but flat and unpleasing to the eye. Seldom exceeding two miles in width — although, as is the case at Drummond's Island, or Taputeouea, they sometimes reach forty in the length of their sweeping curve — but few present a continuous and unbroken stretch of land, for the greater number consist of perhaps two or three score of small islands, divided only by narrow and shallow channels, through which at high water the tide sweeps in from the ocean to the calm waters of the lagoons with amazing velocity. These strips of land, whether broken or continuous, form the eastern or windward boundaries of the lagoons; on the western or lee side lie barrier reefs, between whose jagged coral walls there are, at intervals widely apart, passages sufficiently deep for a thousand-ton ship to pass through in safety, and anchor in the transparent depths of the lagoon within its protecting arms.

. . . . .

Years ago, in the days when the whaleships from Nantucket, and Salem, and Martha's Vineyard, and New Bedford cruised northward towards the cold seas of Japan and Tchantar Bay, and the smoky glare of their tryworks lit up the ocean at night, the Gilberts were a wild place, and many a murderous scene was enacted on white beach and shady palm grove. Time after time some whaler, lying to in fancied security outside the passage of a lagoon, with half her crew ashore intoxicated with sour toddy, and the other half on board unsuspicious of danger, would be attacked by the ferocious brown people. Swimming off at night-time, with knives held between their teeth, a desperate attempt would be made to cut off the ship. Sometimes the attempt succeeded; and then canoe after canoe would put out from the shore, and the wild people, swarming up the ship's side, would tramp about her ensanguined decks and into the cabins seeking for plunder and fiery New England rum. Then, after she had been gutted of everything of value to her captors, as the last canoe pushed off, smoke and then flames would arise, and the burning ship would drift away with the westerly current, and the tragedy of her fate, save to the natives of the island, and perhaps some renegade white man who had stirred them to the deed, would never be known.

. . . . .

In those days—long ere the advent of the first missionary to the isolated equatorial atolls of Polynesia and Melanesia—there were many white men scattered throughout the various islands of the Ellice, Gilbert, and Marshall groups. Men, these, with a past that they cared not to speak of to the few strangers they might chance to meet in their savage retreats. Many were escaped convicts from Van Diemen's Land and New South Wales, living, not in dread of their wild native associates, but in secret terror of recapture by a man-of-war and a return to the horrors of that dreadful past. Casting away the garb of civilisation and tying around their loins the *airiri* or grass girdle of the Gilbert Islanders, they soon became in appearance, manners, language, and thoughts pure natives. For them the outside world meant a life of degradation, possibly a shameful death. And as the years went by and the bitter memories of the black days of old, resonant with the clank of fetters and the warder's harsh cry, became dulled and faint, so died away that once for-ever-haunting fear of discovery and recapture. In Teaké, the bronzed, half-naked savage chief of Maiana, or Mési, the desperate leader of the natives that cut off the barque *Addie Passmore* at Marakei, the identity of such men as "Nuggety" Jack West and Macy O'Shea, once of Van Diemen's Land or Norfolk Island, was lost for ever.

. . . . .

II.

On Kuria, the one beautiful island of the Gilberts, there lived four such white men as those I speak of. Whence they came they alone knew. Two of them—a Portuguese deserter from a whaler and a man named Corton—had been some years on the island when they were joined by two others who came over from Apamama in a boat. One was called Tamu (Tom) by the natives, and from the ease with which he spoke the Gilbert Island dialect and his familiarity with native customs, he had plainly lived many years among the natives; the other was a tall, dark-skinned, and morose-looking man of nearly fifty. He was known as Hari to the natives—once, in that outer world from which some crime had dissevered him for ever, he was Henry Deschard.

Although not familiar with either the language or the customs of the ferocious inhabitants of the Gilbert Group, it was soon seen by the ease with which he acquired both that Hari had spent long years roaming about the islands of the Pacific. In colour he was darker than the Kurians themselves; in his love of the bloodshed and slaughter that so often ran riot in native quarrels he surpassed even the fiercest native; and as he eagerly espoused the cause of any Kurian chief who sought his aid he rapidly became a man of note on the island, and dreaded by the natives elsewhere in the group.

There were then over a thousand people living on Kuria—or rather, on Kuria and Oneaka, for the island is divided by one of those narrow channels before mentioned; and at Oneaka Tamu and Deschard lived, while the Portuguese and the man Corton had long held joint sway with the native chief of Kuria.

During the time the four renegades had lived on the island two vessels that had touched there had had narrow escapes from seizure by the natives. The first of these, a small Hawaiian whaling brig, was attacked when she was lying becalmed between Kuria and Aranuka. A breeze springing up, she escaped after the loss of a boat's crew, who were entrapped on the latter island. In this affair Deschard and Tamu had taken part; in the next—an attempt to capture a sandalwooding barque bound to China—he was leader, with Corton as his associate. The sandalwooder, however, carried a large and well-armed crew, and the treacherous surprise so elaborately planned came to ignominious failure. Deschard accused his fellow-beachcomber of cowardice at a critical moment. The two men became bitter enemies, and for years never spoke to each other.

III.

But one afternoon a sail was sighted standing in for the island, and in their hateful bond of villainy the two men became reconciled, and agreed with Pedro and Tamu and some hundreds of natives to try to decoy the vessel to an anchor and cut her off. The beachcombers, who were tired of living on Kuria, were anxious to get away; the natives desired the plunder to be obtained from the prize. A compact was then made that the ship, after the natives had done with her, was not to be burnt, but was to be handed over to the white men, who were to lead the enterprise.

• • • • •

Sailing slowly along till she came within a mile of the reef, the vessel hove to and lowered a boat. She was a large brigantine, and the murderous beings who watched her from the shore saw with cruel pleasure that she did not appear to carry a large crew.

It had been agreed upon that Corton, who had special aptitude for such work, should meet the boat and endeavour to lure the crew into the interior, under the promise of giving them a quantity of fresh-water fish from the artificial ponds belonging to the chief, while Deschard and the other two, with their body of native allies, should remain at the village on Oneaka, and at the proper moment attack the ship.

As the boat drew near, the officer who was in charge saw that although there were numbers of natives clustered together on the beach, the greater portion were women and children. He had with him five men, all armed with muskets and cutlasses, and although extremely anxious to avoid a collision, he was not at all alarmed. The natives meanwhile preserved a passive attitude, and when the men in the boat, at a word from the officer, stopped rowing, backed her in stern first, and then lay on their oars, they nearly all sat down on the sand and waited for him to speak.

Standing up in the boat, the officer hailed—

"Hallo there, ashore! Any white men living here?"

For a minute or so there was no answer, and the eyes of the natives turned in the direction of one of their number who kept well in the background.

Again the seaman hailed, and then a man, seemingly a native, stout and muscular, with hair falling down in thick masses upon his reddish-brown shoulders, walked slowly out from the others, and folding his brawny arms across his naked chest, he answered—

"Yes; there's some white men here."

The officer, who was the mate of the brigantine, then spoke for a few minutes to a young man who pulled bow oar, and who from his dress was not one of the crew, and said finally, "Well, let us make sure that there is no danger first, Maurice."

The young man nodded, and then the mate addressed the seeming native again:

"There's a young fellow here wants to come ashore; he wants to see one of the white men here. Can he come ashore?"

"Of course he can. D'ye think we're a lot o' cannibals here? I'm a white man myself," and he laughed coarsely; then added quickly, "Who does he want to see?"

The man who pulled the bow oar sprang to his feet.

"I want to see Henry Deschard!"

"Do you?" was the sneering response. "Well, I don't know as you can. This isn't his day at home, like; besides that, he's a good long way from here just now."

"I've got good news for him," urged the man called Maurice.

The beachcomber meditated a few seconds; then he walked down to the boat.

"Look here," he said, "I'm telling the exac' truth. Deschard's place is a long way from here, in the bush too, so you can't go there in the boat; but look here, why can't you chaps come along with me? I'll show you the way, and you'll have a good look at the island. There's nothin' to be afraid of, I can tell you. Why, these natives is that scared of all them guns there that you won't see 'em for dust when you come with me; an' the chief says as you chaps can drag one of his fish-ponds."

The mate was tempted; but his orders were to allow only the man Maurice to land, and to make haste back as soon as his mission was accomplished. Shaking his head to the renegade's wily suggestion, he, however, told Maurice that he could go and endeavour to communicate with Deschard. In the meantime he would return to the ship, and tell the captain—"and the other" (these last words with a look full of meaning at the young man) that everything was going on all right.

Foiled in his plan of inducing all the men to come ashore, Corton assumed a careless manner, and told Maurice that he was still willing to conduct him to Deschard, but that he would not be able to return to the ship that night, as the distance was too great.

The mate was agreeable to this, and bidding the beachcomber and his victim good-day he returned to the ship.

Holding the young man's hand in his, the burly renegade passed through the crowd of silent natives, and spoke to them in their own tongue.

"Hide well thy spears and clubs, my children; 'tis not yet time to act."

Still clasping the hand of his companion, he led the way through the native town, and then into the narrow bush track that led to Oneaka, and in another five minutes they were alone, or apparently so, for nought could be heard in the fast gathering darkness but their own footsteps as they trod the leafy path, and the sound of the breaching surf long miles away.

Suddenly the beachcomber stopped, and in a harsh voice said—

"What is the good news for Deschard?"

"That I cannot tell you," answered the stripling, firmly, though the grim visage, tattooed body, and now threatening aspect of his questioner might well have intimidated even a bolder man, and instinctively he thrust his hand into the bosom of his shirt and grasped a letter he carried there.

"Then neither shall Deschard know it," said the man savagely, and throwing himself upon the young man he bore him to the ground, while shadowy, naked figures glided out from the blackness of the forest and bound and gagged him without a sound. Then carrying him away from the path the natives placed him, without roughness, under the shelter of an empty house, and then left him.

The agony of mind endured by the helpless prisoner may be imagined when, unable to speak or move, he saw the beachcomber and his savage followers vanish into the darkness; for the letter which he carried had been written only a few hours before by the wife of the man Deschard, telling him of her loving quest, and of her and her children's presence on board the brigantine.

IV.

At daylight next morning some native women, passing by the deserted house on their way to work in the *puraka* plantations of Oneaka, saw the figure of the messenger lying dead. One of the women, named Niapó, in placing her hand upon his bosom to feel if he yet breathed, found the letter which had cost him his life. For nearly twenty years she kept possession of it, doubtless from some superstitious motive, and then it was bought from her by a white trader from Apamama, named Randall, by whom it was sent to the Rev. Mr. Damon, the "Sailors' Friend," a well-known missionary in Honolulu. This was the letter:—

My Dear Husband,—It is nearly three years since I got your letter, but I dared not risk writing to you, even if I had known of a ship leaving for the South Seas or the whale fishery. None of the sandalwooding people in Sydney seemed even to know the name of this island (Courier?). My dear husband, I have enough money now, thank God, to end all our troubles. Your letter was brought to me at Parramatta by a sailor—an American, I think. He gave it first to Maurice. I would have rewarded him, but before I could speak to him he had gone. For ten years I have waited and prayed to God to bring us together again. We came to Sydney in the same ship as Major D——, of the 77th. He has always been so good to us, and so has his wife. Nell is sixteen now, Laura eighteen. God grant that I will see you in a few hours. The captain says that he will land us all at one of the places in the Dutch East Indies. I have paid him £100, and am to pay him £100 when you are safely on board. I have been so miserable for the past year, as Major D—— had heard that a man-of-war was searching the islands, and I was in such terrible fear that we would never meet again. Come quickly, and God bless you, my dear husband. Maurice insisted and begged to be allowed to take this to you. He is nineteen years old now, but will not live long—has been a faithful and good lad. Laura is eighteen, and Nell nearly sixteen now. We are now close to Courier,[1] and should see you ere long.—Your loving and now joyful wife,—ANNA DESCHARD.

. . . . .

In the big *maniapa*, or council house, on Oneaka, two hundred armed and naked savages were sitting awaiting the arrival of Corton and his warriors from

---

[1] The native pronunciation of Kuria is like "Courier."—L.B.

Kuria. A little apart from the muttering, excited natives, and seated together, were the man Deschard and the two other beachcombers, Pedro and Tamu.

As Corton and his men filed across the gravelled pathway that led to the *maniapa*, Deschard, followed by the two other white men, at once came out, and the former, with a fierce curse, demanded of Corton what had kept him.

"Couldn't manage to get them ashore," answered the other, sulkily. Then he proceeded to impart the information he had gained as to the ship, her crew, and armament.

"Nine men and one native boy!" said Deschard, contemptuously. He was a tall, lean-looking, black-bearded man, with even a more terrifying and savage appearance than any of his ruffianly partners in crime, tattooed as he was from the back of his neck to his heels in broad, perpendicular lines. As he fixed his keen eyes upon the countenance of Corton his white teeth showed in a cruel smile through his tangled, unkempt moustache.

Calling out the leading chiefs of the cutting-out party, the four desperadoes consulted with them upon their plan of action for the attack upon the brigantine, and then arranged for each man's work and share o the plunder. The white men were to have the ship, but everything that was of value to the natives and not necessary to the working of the ship was to be given to the natives. The muskets, powder, and ball were to be evenly divided between the whites and their allies.

Six of the native chiefs then swore by the names of their deified ancestors to faithfully observe the murderous compact. After the ship was taken they were to help the white men if the ship had anchored to get her under way again.

It was the intention of Deschard and his mates to make for the East Indies, where they would have no trouble in selling the ship to one of the native potentates of that archipelago.

. . . .

At daylight the brigantine, which had been kept under easy sail during the night, was seen to be about four miles from the land, and standing in. Shortly after, two or three canoes, with only a few men in each, put off from the beach at Oneaka and paddled out leisurely towards the ship. When about a mile or so from the shore they ceased paddling, and the captain of the brigantine saw by his glass that they were engaged in fishing.

This was merely a device to inspire confidence in those on board the ship.

In another hour the brigantine passed close to one of the canoes, and a native, well tutored by past masters in the art of treachery in the part he had to play, stood up in the canoe and held out a large fish, and in broken English said it was a present for the captain.

Pleased at such a friendly overture, the captain put the helm down for the canoe to come alongside. Handing the fish up over the side, the giver clambered up himself. The three other natives in the canoe then paddled quietly away as if under no alarm for the safety of their comrade, and resumed their fishing.

As the ship drew into the land the mate called the

captain's attention to some eight or ten more natives who were swimming off to the ship.

"No danger from these people, sir," he remarked; "they are more frightened of us than we of them, I believe; and then look at the women and girls fishing on the reef. When the women come out like that, fearless and open-like, there isn't much to be afraid of."

One by one the natives who were swimming reached the ship, and apparently encouraged by the presence of the man who had boarded the ship from the fishing canoe, they eagerly clambered up on deck, and were soon on the most friendly terms with the crew, especially with one of their own colour, a half-caste native boy from the island of Ambrym, in the New Hebrides, named Maru.

This Maru was the sole survivor of the awful tragedy that followed, and appeared to be well acquainted with the captain's object in calling at Kuria—to pick up the man named Deschard. More than twenty years afterwards, when speaking of the events here narrated, his eyes filled with tears when he told of the "white lady and her two daughters" who were passengers, and who had sat on the poop the previous day awaiting the return of the mate's boat, and for tidings of him whom they had come so far to find.

· · · · ·

V.

The timid and respectful manner of the islanders had now so impressed the master of the brigantine that in a fatal moment he decided to anchor. Telling the mate to range the cable and clear away all ready, he descended to the cabin and tapped at the door of a state-room.

"I am going to anchor, Mrs. Deschard, but as there are a lot of rather curious-looking natives on board, you and the young ladies had better keep to your cabin."

The door opened, and a girl of seventeen or eighteen appeared, and, taking the captain's hand, she whispered—

"She is asleep, captain. She kept awake till daylight, hoping that my father would come in the night. Do you think that anything has happened either to him or Maurice?"

Maru, the Ambrym cabin-boy, said that the captain "patted the girl's hand" and told her to have no fear —that her father was on the island "sure enough," and that Maurice would return with him by breakfast time.

The brigantine anchored close in to the shore, between Kuria and Oneaka, and in a few minutes the long boat was lowered to proceed on shore and bring off Maurice and Deschard. Four hands got into her and then the mate. Just as he was about to cast off, the English-speaking native begged the captain to allow him and the rest of his countrymen to go ashore in the boat. Unsuspicious of treachery from unarmed natives, the captain consented, and they immediately slipped over the side into the boat.

There were thus but four white men left on board —the captain, second mate, two A.B.'s—and the half-caste boy Maru. Arms and ammunition, sufficient for treble the crew the brigantine carried, were on board. In those days the humblest merchant brig voyaging to the East Indies and China coast carried, in addition to small arms, either two or four guns (generally 6-pounders) in case of an attack by pirates. The brigantine was armed with two 6-pounders, and these, so the Ambrym half-caste said, were still loaded with "bags of bullets" when she came to an anchor. Both of the guns were on the main deck amidships.

 . . . . .

Contrary to the wishes of the mate, who appeared to have the most unbounded confidence in the peaceableness of the natives, the captain had insisted upon his boat's crew taking their arms with them.

No sooner had the boat left the vessel than the English-speaking native desired the mate to pull round to the east side of Oneaka, where, he said, the principal village was situated, and whither Maurice had gone to seek Deschard. It must be remembered that this native and those with him were all members of Corton's *clientèle* at Kuria, and were therefore well aware of his treachery in seizing the messenger to Deschard, and that Maurice had been seized and bound the previous night.

In half an hour, when the boat was hidden from the view of those on board the brigantine, the natives, who outnumbered the whites two to one, at a signal from their leader suddenly threw themselves upon the unsuspecting seamen who were rowing and threw every one of them overboard. The mate, a small, active man, managed to draw a heavy horse pistol from his belt, but ere he could pull the trigger he was dealt a crushing blow with a musket stock. As he fell a native thrust him through and through with one of the seamen's cutlasses. As for the unfortunate seamen, they were killed one by one as they struggled in the water. That part of the fell work accomplished, the natives pulled the boat in towards Oneaka, where some ten or fifteen large native double-ended boats and canoes, all filled with savages lusting for blood and rapine, awaited them.

Deschard, a man of the most savage courage, was in command of some twenty or thirty of the most noted of the Oneaka warriors; and on learning from Tebarian (the native who spoke English and who was Corton's brown familiar) that the two guns were in the waist of the ship, he instructed his white comrades to follow in the wake of his boat, and, once they got alongside, board the ship wherever their fancy dictated.

There was a muttered *E rairai!* (Good!) of approval from the listening natives, and then in perfect silence and intuitive discipline the paddles struck the water, and the boat and canoes, with their naked, savage crews, sped away on their mission of death.

VI.

But, long before they imagined, they had been discovered, and their purpose divined from the ship. Maru, the keen-eyed half-caste, who was the first to notice their approach, knew from the manner in which the canoes kept together that something unusual was about to occur, and instantly called the captain. Glass in hand, the latter ascended the main rigging for a dozen ratlins or so and looked at the advancing flotilla. A very brief glance told him that the boy had good cause for alarm—the natives intended to cut off the ship, and the captain, whom Maru described as "an old man with a white head," at once set about to make such a defence as the critical state of affairs rendered possible.

Calling his men to him and giving them muskets, he posted two of them on top of the deckhouse, and with the remainder of his poor force stationed himself upon the poop. With a faint hope that they might yet be intimidated from attacking, he fired a musket shot in the direction of the leading boat. No notice was taken; so, descending to the main deck with his men, he ran out one of the 6-pounders and fired it. The roar of the heavily-charged gun was answered by a shrill yell of defiance from two hundred throats.

"Then," said Maru, "the captain go below and say good-bye to women and girls, and shut and lock cabin door."

Returning to the deck, the brave old man and his second mate and two men picked up their muskets and began to fire at the black mass of boats and men that were now well within range. As they fired, the boy Maru loaded spare muskets for them as fast as his trembling hands would permit.

Once only, as the brigantine swung to the current, the captain brought the gun on the port side to bear on them again, and fired; and again there came back the same appalling yell of defiance, for the shower of bullets only made a wide slat of foam a hundred yards short of the leading boat.

By the time the gun was reloaded the brigantine had swung round head to shore again; and then, as the despairing but courageous seamen were trying to drag it forward again, Deschard and his savages in the leading boat had gained the ship, and the wild figure of the all but naked beachcomber sprang on deck, followed by his own crew and nearly two hundred other fiends well-nigh as bloodthirsty and cruel as himself. Some two or three of them had been killed by the musketry fire from the ship, and their fellows needed no incentive from their white leaders to slay and spare not.

Abandoning the gun, the captain and his three men and the boy Maru succeeded in fighting their way through Deschard's savages and reaching one of the cabin doors, which, situated under the break of the high poop, opened to the main deck. Ere they could all gain the shelter of the cabin and secure the door the second mate and one of the seamen were cut down and ruthlessly slaughtered, and of the three that did, one—the remaining seaman—was mortally wounded and dying fast.

Even at such a moment as this, hardened and merciless as were their natures and blood-stained their past, it cannot be thought that had Deschard and his co-pirates known that white women were on board the brigantine they would have perpetrated their last dreadful deed. In his recital of the final scene in the cabin Maru spoke of the white woman and the two girls coming out of their state-room and kneeling down and praying with their arms clasped around each other's waists. Surely the sound of their dying prayers could never have been heard by Deschard when, in the native tongue, he called out for one of the guns to be run aft.

• • • • •

"By and by," said Maru, "woman and girl come to captain and sailor-man Charlie and me and cry and say good-bye, and then captain he pray too. Then he get up and take cutlass, and sailor-man Charlie he take cutlass too, but he too weak and fall down; so captain say, 'Never mind, Charlie, you and me die now like men.'"

Then, cutlass in hand, the white-haired old skipper stood over the kneeling figures of the three women and waited for the end. And now the silence was broken by a rumbling sound, and then came a rush of naked feet along the deck.

"It is the gun," said Maru to the captain, and in an agony of terror he lifted up the hatch of the lazarette under the cabin table and jumped below. And then Deschard's voice was heard.

"*Ta mai te ae*" (Give me the fire).

A blinding flash, a deafening roar, and splintering and crashing of timber followed, and as the heavy pall of smoke lifted, Deschard and the others looked in at their bloody work, shuddered, and turned away.

Pedro, the Portuguese, his dark features turned to a ghastly pallor, was the only one of the four men who had courage enough to assist some of the natives in removing from the cabin the bodies of the three poor creatures who, but such a short time before, were full of happiness and hope. Deschard and the three others, after that one shuddering glance, had kept away from the vicinity of the shot-torn cabin.

. . . . .

VII.

The conditions of the cutting off of the brigantine were faithfully observed by the contracting parties, and long ere night fell the last boatload of plunder had been taken ashore. Tebarau, chief of Oneaka, had with his warriors helped to heave up anchor, and the vessel, under short canvas, was already a mile or two away from the land, and in his hiding-place in the gloomy lazarette the half-caste boy heard Corton and Deschard laying plans for the future.

Only these two were present in the cabin; Pedro was at the wheel, and Tamu somewhere on deck. Presently Corton brought out the dead captain's despatch box, which they had claimed from the natives, and the two began to examine the contents. There was a considerable amount of money in gold and silver, as well as the usual ship's papers, &c. Corton, who could scarcely read, passed these over to his companion, and then ran his fingers gloatingly through the heap of money before him.

With a hoarse, choking cry and horror-stricken eyes Deschard sprang to his feet, and with shaking hand held out a paper to Corton.

"My God! my God!" exclaimed the unhappy wretch, and sinking down again he buried his face in his hands.

Slowly and laboriously his fellow ex-convict read the document through to the end. It was an agreement to pay the captain of the brigantine the sum of one hundred pounds sterling provided that Henry Deschard was taken on board the brigantine at

Woodle's Island (the name Kuria was known by to whaleships and others), the said sum to be increased to two hundred pounds "provided that Henry Deschard, myself, and my two daughters are landed at Batavia or any other East India port within sixty days from leaving the said island," and was signed ANNA DESCHARD.

Staggering to his feet, the man sought in the ruined and plundered state-room for further evidence. Almost the first objects that he saw were two hanging pockets made of duck—evidently the work of some seaman—bearing upon them the names of "Helen" and "Laura."

. . . . .

Peering up from his hiding-place in the lazarette, where he had lain hidden under a heap of old jute bagging and other débris, Maru saw Deschard return to the cabin and take up a loaded musket. Sitting in the captain's chair, and leaning back, he placed the muzzle to his throat and touched the trigger with his naked foot. As the loud report rang out, and the cabin filled with smoke, the boy crawled from his dark retreat, and, stepping over the prostrate figure of Deschard, he reached the deck and sprang overboard.

For hours the boy swam through the darkness towards the land, guided by the lights of the fires that in the Gilbert and other equatorial islands are kindled at night-time on every beach. He was picked up by a fishing party, and probably on account of his youth and exhausted condition his life was spared.

That night as he lay sleeping under a mat in the

big *maniapa* on Kuria he was awakened by loud cries, and looking seaward he saw a bright glare away to the westward.

It was the brigantine on fire.

Launching their canoes, the natives went out to her, and were soon close enough to see that she was burning fiercely from for'ard to amidships, and that her three boats were all on board—two hanging to the davits and one on the deckhouse. But of the four beachcombers there was no sign.

Knowing well that no other ship had been near the island, and that therefore the white men could not have escaped by that means without being seen from the shore, the natives, surmising that they were in a drunken sleep, called loudly to them to awake; but only the roaring of the flames broke the silence of the ocean. Not daring to go nearer, the natives remained in the vicinity till the brigantine was nothing but a mastless, glowing mass of fire.

Towards midnight she sank; and the last of the beachcombers of Kuria sank with her.

NELL OF MULLINER'S CAMP

Nell of Mulliner's Camp.

MULLINER'S CAMP, on the Hodgkinson, was the most hopeless-looking spot in the most God-forsaken piece of country in North Queensland, and Haughton, the amalgamator at the "Big Surprise" crushing-mill, as he turned wearily away from the battery-tables to look at his "retorting" fire, cursed silently but vigorously at his folly in staying there.

It was Saturday night, and the deadly melancholy of Mulliner's was, if possible, somewhat accentuated by the crash and rattle of the played-out old five-head battery, accompanied by the wheezings and groanings of its notoriously unreliable pumping-gear. Half a mile away from the decrepid old battery, and situated on the summit of an adder-infested ironstone ridge, the dozen or so of bark humpies that constituted Mulliner's Camp proper stood out clearly in the bright starlight in all their squat ugliness. From the extra display of light that shone from the doorway of the largest and most dilapidated-looking of the huts, Haughton knew that the Cooktown mailman had come in, and was shouting a drink for the landlord of the "Booming Nugget" before eating his supper of corned beef and damper and riding onward. For

Mulliner's had gone to the bad altogether; even the beef that the mailman was eating came from a beast belonging to old Channing, of Calypso Downs, which had fallen down a shaft the previous night. Perhaps this matter of a fairly steady beef supply was the silver lining to the black cloud of misfortune that had so long enshrouded the spirits of the few remaining diggers that still clung tenaciously to the duffered-out mining camp, for whenever Mulliner's ran out of meat a beast of Channing's would always—by some mysterious dispensation of a kindly goldfield's Providence—fall down a shaft and suffer mortal injuries.

. . . . .

Just at the present moment Haughton, as he threw a log or two into the retort furnace and watched the shower of sparks fly high up over the battery roof, was thinking of old Channing's daughter Kate, and the curious state of affairs existing between her and his partner Ballantyne. Briefly stated, this is what had occurred—that is, as far as Haughton knew.

. . . . .

Twelve months before, Mrs. Channing, a meek-faced, religious-minded lady, had succumbed to the worries of life under the combined and prostrating influences of a galvanised iron roof, an independent Chinaman cook, and a small powerful theological library. Immediately after her death, old Channing at once wrote to his daughter, then at school in Sydney, to come back "and cheer up his lonely life."

"Poor dad," said Kate, "I suppose he means for me to continue poor mother's feeble remonstrances to Chow Kum about giving away so much rations to the station gins, and to lend a hand when we muster for branding."

However, being a dutiful girl, she packed up and went.

On board the steamer she had met Ballantyne, who was returning to Queensland to resume his mining pursuits in the Palmer District. He knew old Channing well by reputation as a wealthy but eccentric old squatter, and in a few days he managed to make the girl fall violently in love with him. The day that the steamer reached Brisbane a telegram was brought on board for Miss Channing. It was from her father, telling her that Mrs. Lankey, of Mount Brindlebul, was coming up from Sydney in another week, and she was to wait in Brisbane for her. Then they were to travel northward together.

If there was one woman in the world she hated it was Mrs. Lankey, of Mount Brindlebul station, in the Gulf country, and Ballantyne, from whom she could hide nothing, saw his opportunity, and took it. He took her ashore, placed her in lodgings, went to an hotel himself, and the day before her future escort arrived, married her.

Perfectly satisfied with the cogent reasons he gave for secrecy in not apprising her father of their marriage, and shedding tears at the nonchalant manner in which he alluded to a honeymoon "some time in a year or so when the old man comes to know of it," pretty Kate Channing went back alone to her lodgings to await Mrs. Lankey and cogitate upon the peculiarly masterful way in which Ballantyne had wooed and won her.

· · · · ·

Six months afterwards she got a letter from Ballantyne, telling her that he had bought Petermann's crushing mill at Mulliner's Camp, "so as to be near you, my pet," he said. At the same time he warned her of the folly of their attempting to meet, at least openly; but added that Haughton, his partner, who knew of his marriage, would visit Calypso Downs occasionally and give her news of him; also that they could correspond by the same medium.

Thus matters stood between them for some months, till Kate, wearying to meet the cold, calculating Ballantyne, adopted the device of riding over late every Sunday afternoon to Mulliner's for the mail, instead of her father sending over one of his black boys.

But instead of meeting her with kisses, Ballantyne terrified her with savage reproaches. It was madness, he said, for her to run such a risk. By and by he would be in a better position; at present he was as poor as a rat, and it was best for them to be apart. And Kate, thoroughly believing in him, bent to his will. She knew that her father was, as Ballantyne thoughtfully observed, such a violent-tempered old man that he would cast her off utterly unless he was "managed" properly when he learnt of her marriage.

"And don't come down this way from Mulliner's," added the careful Ballantyne. "There's an old mail tin, about a mile or so away from here, near the worked-out alluvial patch. You can always drop a letter in there for me. Haughton's such a good-natured ass that he'll play Mercury for you. Anyway, I'll send him to look in the tin every Sunday night."

That, so far, was the history of Mr. and Mrs. Ballantyne.

．　　　．　　　．　　　．　　　．

"Another duffing crushing," muttered Haughton, as he stooped and placed his hand into the bucket of quicksilver under the nozzle of the retort pipe. "What between a reef that doesn't pan out five pennyweights to the ton, and a woman that pans out too rich, I'm sick of the cursed place."

As he stood up again, and, hands on his hips, looked moodily into the fire, a woman came down the rough path leading from Ballantyne's house to the battery. Walking quickly across the lighted space that intervened between the blacksmith's forge and the fire, she placed a billy of tea on the brick furnace-wall, and then turned her handsome black-browed, gipsy-like face up to his. This was Nell Lawson, the woman who had "panned out too rich."

"Here's your tea, Dick," she said.

"Thanks," he said, taking it from her, and then with a quick look over towards the battery, "I wish you wouldn't call me 'Dick' when any of the hands are about; Lawson might hear of it, and I don't want you to get into any trouble over me."

The black eyes sparkled, and the smooth olive-hued features flushed darkly in the firelight as she grasped his arm.

"You lie!" and she set her teeth. "A lot you care! Do you think I'm a silly? Do you think as I don't know that you want to sling me and don't know how to go about it?" and she grasped his arm savagely.

Haughton looked at her in gloomy silence for a few

seconds. Standing there, face to face, they looked so alike in features—he wiry, muscular, black-bearded, and bronzed to the hue of an Arab, and she tall, dark-haired, with oval, passionate face—they might have been taken for brother and sister.

She let his arm free, and then, being only a working miner's wife, and possessing no handkerchief, whipped her apron to her eyes.

"You're a damned cur!" she said, chokingly. "If it hadn't ha' been for you I'd ha' gone along all right wi' Bob, and put up wi' livin' in this place; an' now——"

"Look here, Nell," said Haughton, drawing her away into the shadow of the forge, "I'm a cur, as you say; but I'd be a worse cur to keep on this way. You can't marry me, can you?"

"You used to talk about our boltin'—*once*," and she snapped out the last word.

Haughton tried to explain why the "bolting" so trenchantly referred to did not eventuate. He was stone-broke. Ballantyne was going to do his own amalgamating at the battery, and it would be cruel of him to ask her to share his fortunes. (Here he began to appreciate his leaning to morality.) If she was a single girl he would stay at Mulliner's and fight it out with bad luck for her sake; but they couldn't go on like this any more. And the people at Mulliner's were beginning to talk about them, &c., &c.

She heard him in silence, and then gave a short, jarring laugh—the laugh that ought to tell a man that he is no longer believed in—by a woman who has loved him.

"I know," she said, quietly, "you want to get clear

o' me. You're took up with Kate Channing, the *proper* Miss Channing that rides over here o' Sundays to meet you on the sly."

At first he meant to undeceive her, then he thought, "What does it matter? I'll be away from here in a day or so, and after I've gone she'll find I'm not so base as she thought me, poor girl;" so, looking away from her so as to avoid the dangerous light that gleamed in her passionate eyes, he made the plunge.

"That's it, Nell. I'm hard up and desperate. If you were a free woman——"

She struck him in the mouth with her clenched hand—"I'll kill her first, Dick Haughton," and then left him.

. . . . .

A mile or so out from the battery, on a seldom used track that led to an abandoned alluvial workings, a stained and weather-worn biscuit-tin had been nailed to an iron-bark tree. In the prosperous days of Mulliner's it had been placed there by the diggers as a receptacle for letters, and its location there saved the mailman a long *détour* to their camp. At present poor loving Kate Channing and Dick Haughton were the only persons who ever looked into it. After getting the station letters from the landlord of the "Booming Nugget," Kate would ride through the bush and come out on the track just opposite; then, bending down from her horse, she would peer eagerly into the tin to see if a letter had been left there for her. Generally there was not. So, with a sad, wistful look in her blue eyes, she would drop her own tenderly-worded letter in and ride away home.

Twice Nell Lawson had seen her passing over the

ridge towards the old workings, and had wondered what had taken her so far off the road; and on each of these occasions she had seen Dick Haughton follow in the same direction shortly after. He was never away more than half an hour. The first time she simply wondered, the next she grew suspicious, and as she saw him returning went and stopped him. As she threw her arms around his neck she felt the rustling of a letter that lay loosely in the front of the dungaree jumper he always wore when at work. She said nothing, but determined to watch, and one day, with the bitterest hatred gathering at her heart, she saw Kate Channing ride up to the tin on the iron-bark, look carefully inside, and then drop in a letter. And as Nell Lawson could not read she let it lay there untouched. But from that hour murder lay in her passionate heart.

That evening, as she entered Bob Lawson's humpy, her husband, a big, heavy-featured man, looked up and saw the ghastly pallor of her face.

"Why, what's the matter wi' 'ee, Nell? You be lookin' quite sick-loike lately. Tell 'ee what, Nell, thee wants a cheange."

"Mulliner's be a dull pleace," she answered, mechanically.

"Aye, lass, dull as hell in a fog. Mebbe I'll take thee somewheres for a spell."

. . . . .

For nearly another week she nursed her hatred and planned her revenge; and Haughton, as he saw the dark rings forming under her eyes, and the cold, listless manner as she went about her work, began to experience a higher phase of feeling for her than that of the mere passion which her beauty had first awakened in him long months before.

* * * * *

It was five o'clock on Sunday afternoon. The fierce, blinding sun had just disappeared behind the hideous basalt range twenty miles away from the "Big Surprise," when Nell Lawson put on her white sun-hood and walked slowly towards the old alluvial workings. When well out of sight from any one, near the battery, she turned off towards the creek and made for a big Leichhardt tree that stood on the bank. Underneath it, and evidently waiting for her, was a black fellow, a truculent-looking runaway trooper named Barney.

"You got him that fellow Barney?" she asked, in a low voice.

"*Yo ai*," he replied, keeping one hand behind his back. "Where that plenty fellow money you yabber me yesterday?"

"Here," and she showed him some silver; "ten fellow shilling."

Barney grinned, took the money, and then handed her an old broken-handled crockery teapot, which, in place of a lid, was covered over with a strip of ti-tree bark, firmly secured to the bottom by a strip of dirty calico.

As soon as the black fellow had gone she picked up that which he had given her and walked quickly along the track till she reached the old mail tin. She stood awhile and listened. Not a sound disturbed the heated, oppressive silence. Placing the teapot on the ground, she lifted the stiff, creaking lid of the tin and pushed it well back. Then, taking up the teapot again, she placed one hand firmly upon the ti-tree bark covering the top, while with the other she unfastened the strip of rag that kept it in position. In another moment, grasping the broken spout in her left hand, she held it over the open tin, and, with a rapid motion, turned it upside down, and whipped away her right hand from the piece of bark.

Something fell heavily against the bottom of the tin, and in an instant she slammed down the lid, and threw the empty teapot in among the boulders, where it smashed to pieces. Then, an evil smile on her dark face, she placed her ear to the side of the tin and listened. A faint, creeping, crawling sound was all she heard. In another minute, with hand pressed tightly against her wildly beating heart, she fled homewards.

· · · · ·

"This will be my last ride over, dear Ted," was the beginning of the letter to Ballantyne that lay in Channing's bosom. "Father is very ill, and I cannot leave him. Do let me tell him, and ask his forgiveness; it is so miserable for me to keep up this deceit."

Darkness had set in by the time she had got the mail from the landlord of the "Booming Nugget," and turned her horse's head into the track that led over the ridge to the old workings.

· · · · ·

Two hours before daylight, Kate Channing's horse walked riderless up to the sliprails of Calypso Downs, and the stockman who had kept awake awaiting her return, went out to let his young mistress in.

"Got throwed somewhere, I suppose," he grumbled,

after examining the horse. "This is a nice go. It's no use telling the old man about it; he's too sick to be worried just now, anyway."

Taking a black boy with him, and leading Kate's horse, he set out to look for her, expecting, unless she was hurt, to meet her somewhere between the station and Mulliner's Camp. Just as daylight broke, the black boy, who was leading, stopped.

"Young missus been tumble off horse here," and he pointed to where the scrubby undergrowth on one side of the track was crushed down and broken.

The stockman nodded. "Horse been shy I think it, Billy, at that old fellow post-office there?" and he pointed to the old mail tin, which was not ten feet from where Billy said she had fallen off.

"Go ahead, Billy," said the stockman, "I believe young missus no catch him horse again, and she walk along to Mulliner's."

"*Yo ai*," answered the black boy, and he started ahead. In a few minutes he stopped again with a puzzled look and pointed to Kate Channing's tracks.

"Young missus been walk about all same drunk."

"By jingo, she's got hurted, I fear," said the stockman. "Push ahead, Billy."

A hundred yards further on they found her dead, lying face downwards on the track.

Lifting her cold, stiffened body in his arms, the stockman carried his burden along to Ballantyne's house. Haughton met him at the door. Together they laid the still figure upon the sofa in the front room, and then while the stockman went for Nell Lawson, Haughton went to Ballantyne's bunk and awoke and told him. His mouth twitched nervously for a second or two, and then his hard, impassive nature asserted itself again.

* * * *

"'Tis a terrible thing this, Ballantyne," said Haughton, sympathetically, as they walked out together to see the place where she had been thrown.

"Yes," assented the other, "dreadful. Did you hear what Channing's black boy told me?"

"No!"

"He says that she has died from snake-bite. I believe him, too. I saw a boy die on the Etheridge from snake-bite, and he looked as she does now; besides that, there is not a scratch or bruise on her body, so she couldn't have received any hurt unless it was an internal one when she was thrown. Here's the place," and then he started back, for lying at the foot of the tree was the panting, trembling figure of Nell Lawson.

She had tried to get there before them to efface all traces of her deadly work.

"What are you doing here, Mrs. Lawson?" said Ballantyne, sharply; "we sent over for you; don't you know what has happened?"

The strange hysterical "yes" that issued from her pallid lips caused Ballantyne to turn his keen grey eyes upon her intently. Then something of the truth must have flashed across his mind, for he walked up to the tree and looked into the tin.

"Good God!" he said, "poor little woman!" and then he called to Haughton. "Come here, and see what killed her!"

Haughton looked, and a deadly horror chilled his blood: lying in the bottom of the tin was a thick, brownish-red death adder. It raised its hideous, flatted head for a moment, then lowered it, and lay there regarding them with its deadly eye.

"How did it get there?" he asked.

Ballantyne pointed to Nell Lawson, who now stood and leant against a tree for support.

Haughton sprang to her side and seized her hands.

"Are you a murderess, Nell? What had she done to you that you should take her innocent life? She was nothing to me—she was Ballantyne's wife."

She looked at him steadily, and her lips moved, then a shrill, horrible laugh burst forth, and she fell unconscious at his feet.

That day Haughton left Mulliner's Camp for ever.

· · · · ·

Perhaps this story should have another ending, and Nell Lawson have met with a just retribution. But, as is the case of many other women—and men—with natures such as hers, she did not. For when old Channing lay dying she nursed him tenderly to the last, and perhaps because of this, or for that he could never understand why blue-eyed Kate had never come back, he left her all he had, much to the wondering admiration of honest, dull-witted Bob, her husband, who almost immediately after the old man's death, when returning home one night from the "Booming Nugget," filled with a great peace of mind and a considerable quantity of bad rum, fell down a shaft and broke his neck, after the manner of one of old Channing's bullocks—and then she married Ballantyne.

Everything seems to come to him who waits— especially if he is systematic in his villainy, and has a confiding wife—as had Ballantyne in his first matrimonial venture.

AURIKI REEF

Auriki Reef.

ONE evening, not long ago, an old island comrade and I sat on the verandah looking out upon the waters of Sydney Harbour, smoking and talking of the old wild days down there in the Marshall group, among the brown people who dwell on the white beaches under the shade of the swaying palms. And as we talked, the faces of those we had known came back one by one to our memories, and passed away.

· · · · ·

In front of us, with her tall, black spars cutting out clearly against the flood of moonlight, that lit up the waters of the quiet little bay, lay the old *Wolverene*—to both of us a silent reminder of one night not long ago, under far-off skies, when the old corvette sailed past our little schooner, towering up above us, a cloud of spotless white canvas, as she gracefully rose and sank to the long sweep of the ocean swell.

· · · · ·

"Poor old Tierney," said my friend, alluding to the captain of that little schooner. "He's dead now; blew his hand off with dynamite down in the Gilbert Group—did you know?"

"Yes. What a good fellow he was! There are few like him left now. Aye, few indeed."

"By the way, did he ever tell you about Jack Lester and his little daughter, Tessa?"

"Something of it. You were with him in the *Mana* that trip, weren't you?"

. . . . .

"Yes," said my friend, "Brayley and I both. He had been up to Honolulu, sick; and he came on board of the *Mana*, and seemed so anxious to get back to his station on Maduro that Tierney—good old fellow as he was—told him to bring his traps aboard, and he would land him there on the way to Samoa. His wife had died five years before, and he had to leave his station in the care of his daughter, a child of twelve or so. Not that he fretted much about the station—it was only the little girl he thought of."

We smoked on in silence awhile. Then my friend resumed—

"I shall never forget that voyage. It was a night such as this that it happened—I mean that affair of the boat on Auriki Reef."

Fifteen years ago is a long time to try back, and although I had been told something of a strange incident that had occurred during one voyage of the Hawaiian schooner *Mana* (she is now a Sydney collier), I could not recall the circumstances.

So then my friend told me the story of the boat on Auriki Reef.

. . . . .

"I have told you that Brayley was a man of few words. But sometimes as we paced the deck together at night, as the schooner skimmed over the seas before the lusty trade-wind, he would talk to me of his child;

and it was easy for me to see that his love for her was the one hope of his life.

"'I am going back to England soon,' he said to me one night; 'there is but one of us left—my sister—and I would like to see her face again in this world. She is older than I—she is past fifty now.... And it is thirty years since I said good-bye to her ... thirty years ... thirty long years,' and then he turned his face away and looked out upon the sea. 'Just to see her, and then say good-bye again, for here I have cast my lot, and here I will die. If I were alone in the world perhaps I would take to civilisation again, but Tessa'—he shook his head—'she would wither and die in cold England.'

. . . . .

"Ten days out we ran in amongst the Radack Chain of the Marshall Islands, and the wind falling light, and being surrounded by reefs and low uninhabited coral atolls, Tierney brought to, and anchored for the night. You know the spot, about nine miles due west of Ailuk, and between two sandy atolls covered with a scant growth of cocoanuts and pandanus palms.

. . . . .

"The ship being all right the hands turned in, leaving only one man on watch, while we three white men laid down aft to smoke and yarn. It was a bright moonlight night, as light as day—just such a night as this. Away on our port quarter, distant about a quarter of a mile, was a shallow patch on which the surf was breaking. It was merely one of those flat patches of coral that, rising up steep from the bottom, have deep water all round them, but are always covered on the surface by a depth of one or two fathoms—'mushrooms,' we call them, you know. Well, it was such a wonderfully clear night that that shallow patch, with the surf hissing and swirling over and around it, was as clearly visible to us on the schooner as if it had been under our counter, not ten feet away.

. . . . .

"Covering up my face from the vivid moonlight with a soft native mat, I laid down, and after awhile dropped off to sleep.

"How long I had been asleep I did not know then—I learnt afterwards that it was nearly four hours—when I was awakened by a loud hail of 'Boat ahoy!' called out by some one on board.

"I was awake in an instant, and sprang to my feet.

"'What is it?' I said to Tierney and Brayley, who were standing close to me, looking out towards the breaking reef. 'Where is the boat that you are hailing?'

"Neither of them answered; Tierney, turning towards me for a second, made a curious half-commanding, half-imploring gesture as if to ask my silence, and then gripping Brayley by his shoulder, stared wildly at the white seeth of the breakers astern of us.

"A quick look along the decks for'ard showed me that all the native sailors were on deck and clustered together in the waist, as far aft as they dared come. Each man had hold of his fellow, and with open mouths and wildly staring eyes they stood like statues of bronze, in an attitude of horror and amazement.

"'What is it?' I commenced again, when Tierney

slowly raised his clenched and shaking hand and touched me.

"'Look,' he said, in a strange, quivering whisper, 'in the name of God, man, what is that?'

·   ·   ·   ·   ·

"I followed the direction of his shaking hand. It pointed along the broad, golden stream of moonlight that ran from close under our stern right across to the low, black line that we knew was Ailuk Island. For a moment I saw nothing, then, suddenly, amid the wild boil of the surf in Auriki, I saw a boat, a white-painted boat with a black gunwale streak. One person seemed to be sitting aft with his face drooping upon his breast. The boat seemed to me to be in the very centre of the wild turmoil of waters, and yet to ride with perfect ease and safety. Presently, however, I saw that it was on the other side of the reef, yet so close that the back spray from the curling rollers must have fallen upon it.

·   ·   ·   ·   ·

"Pushing Captain Tierney away from him, Brayley suddenly seemed to straighten himself, and taking a step in advance of us he again hailed—

"'Boat, ahoy!'

"The loud, hoarse cry pealed over the waters, but no answer came from the silent figure, and then Brayley turned towards us. His bronzed features had paled to the hue of death, and for a moment or two his mouth twitched.

"'For God's sake, Tierney, call the hands and lower the boat. It is nothing from the other world that we see—*it is my daughter, Tessa.*'

"In a second the old man sprang into life and action, and in a shrill voice that sounded like a scream he called, 'Man the boat, lads!'

"Before one could have counted twenty the boat was in the water, clear of the falls, and Tierney and Brayley, with a crew of four natives, were pulling swiftly for the other boat.

* * * * *

"In a few minutes they reached her, just as a big roller had all but got her and carried her right on top of Auriki. I saw Brayley get out of our boat and into the other, and lift the sitting figure up in his arms, and then Tierney made fast a line, took the strange boat in tow, and headed back for the ship.

"When the boat was within speaking distance, Tierney hailed me—

"'Get some brandy ready—she is alive.'

* * * * *

"We carried her into the cabin, and as Brayley bent his face over the poor, wasted figure of his child, the hot tears ran down his cheeks, and Tierney whispered to me, 'She is dying fast.'

"We all knew that as soon as we looked at her. Already the grey shadows were deepening on the face of the wanderer as we gathered around her, speaking in whispers. Suddenly the loud clamour of the ship's bell, struck by an unthinking sailor, made the girl's frame quiver.

"With a look of intense pity the captain motioned to Brayley to raise her head to try and get her to swallow a teaspoonful of water. Tenderly the trader raised her, and then for a moment or two the closed, weary eyelids slowly drew back and she gazed into his face.

"'Thank God,' the captain said, 'she knows you, Brayley.'

"A faint, flickering smile played about her lips and then ceased. Then a long, low sigh, and her head fell upon his breast.

. . . . .

"At daylight we hove-up anchor and stood on our course for Brayley's Station on Arhnu. Just as we rounded the south end of Ailuk Island we saw the *Lahaina*, schooner, lying-to and signalling that she wanted to speak. Her skipper came aboard, and hurriedly shaking hands with us, asked if we knew that Jack Brayley's little Tessa had gone adrift in his boat ten days ago.

"Silently Tierney led him to the open skylight and pointed down to where she lay with her father kneeling beside her.

"'Poor man!' said the skipper of the *Lahaina*. 'I'm real sorry. I heerd from the natives that Tessa and two native girls and a boy took the whaleboat, for a joke like, and she said she was going to meet her father, as she had seen him in her sleep, an' she reckoned he was close to on the sea somewhere. I guess the poor thing's got swept to leeward by the current. They had a sail in the boat.'

"'Aye,' said Tierney, 'a squall must have struck the boat and carried away the mast; it was snapped off short about a foot above the thwart.'

. . . . .

"When we ran into Maduro Lagoon three days

afterwards our flag was half-mast high for Tessa Brayley, and for her father as well—for we had found him the next morning on his knees beside her, cold and stiff in death, with his dead hand clasped around hers."

AT THE EBBING OF THE TIDE

At the Ebbing of the Tide.

BLACK TOM'S "hell" was one of the institutions of Samoa. And not an unpleasant hell to look at—a long, rambling, one-storeyed, white-painted wooden building, hidden on the beach side from ships entering Apia Harbour by a number of stately cocoanuts; and as you came upon it from the palm-shaded track that led from the brawling little Vaisigago towards the sweeping curve of Matautu Point, the blaze of scarlet hibiscus growing within the white-paled garden fence gave to this sailors' low drinking-den an inviting appearance of sweetest Arcadian simplicity.

That was nineteen years ago. If you walk along the Matautu path now and ask a native to show you where Tom's house stood, he will point to a smooth, grass-covered bank extending from the right-hand side of the path to the coarse, black sand of Matautu beach. And, although many of the present white residents of the Land of the Treaty Powers have heard of Black Tom, only a few grizzled old traders and store-keepers, relics of the bygone lively days, can talk to you about that grim deed of one quiet night in September.

•   •   •   •   •

Tamasi Uliuli (Black Thomas), as he was called by the natives, had come to Samoa in the fifties, and, after an eventful and varied experience in other portions of the group, had settled down to business in Matautu as a publican, baker and confectioner, butcher, seamen's crimp, and interpreter. You might go all over the Southern States, from St. Augustine to Galveston, and not meet ten such splendid specimens of negro physique and giant strength as this particular coloured gentleman. Tom had married a Samoan woman—Inusia—who had borne him three children, two daughters and one son. Of this latter I have naught to say here, save that the story of *his* short life and tragic end is one common enough to those who have had any experience of a trader's life among the betel-chewing savages of fever-haunted New Britain. And the eldest daughter may also "stand out" of this brief tale.

· · · · ·

Luisa was black. There was no doubt about that. But she was also comely; and her youthful, lissom figure as she walked with springy step to the bathing-place at the Vaisigago gave her a striking individuality among the lighter-coloured Samoan girls who accompanied her. Yet to all of us who lived in Matautu the greatest charms of this curly-haired half-caste were the rich, sweet voice and gay laugh that brightened up her dark-hued countenance as we passed her on the path and returned her cheerful "Talofa, *alii!*" with some merry jest. And, although none of us had any inclination to go into her father's pub. and let *him* serve us with a bottle of Pilsener, Luisa's laughing face and curly head generally had attraction enough to secure, in the course of the day, a good many half-dollars for the 50lb. beef-keg which was Black Tom's treasury.

* * * * *

It gave us a shock one day to see Luisa emerging from the mission chapel with a white-haired old man by her side—married. The matter had been arranged very quietly. For about two months previously this ancient had been one of Black Tom's boarders. He was from New Zealand, and had come to Samoa to invest his money in trade, and being, perhaps, of a retiring and quiet disposition the sight of Mr. Thomas Tilton's innocent-looking dwelling attracted him thither. Anyhow, old Dermott remained there, and it was noticeable that, from the day of his arrival, Tamasi Uliuli exacted the most rigid performance of morning and evening devotions by his family, and that the nightly scenes of riot and howling drunkenness, that had theretofore characterised the "hotel," had unaccountably toned down. In fact, burly old Alvord, the consular interpreter, who had been accustomed to expostulate with Tom for the number of prostrate figures, redolent of bad rum, lying outside on the path in the early morning, showing by the scarcity of their attire that they had been "gone through" by thieving natives, expressed the opinion that Tom was either going mad, or "was getting consairned" about his sinful soul.

* * * * *

The knowledge of the fact that old Dermott had so much worldly wealth stowed away in his camphor-wood trunk, may have had (doubtless it did) the effect of causing this remarkable change in Tom's daily conduct. Dermott, in his way, was sourly religious; and, although not understanding a word of Samoan, was fond of attending the native church at Apia—always in the wake of Luisa, Toĕ-o-le-Sasa, and other young girls. His solemn, wrinkled visage, with deep-set eyes, ever steadily fixed upon the object of his affection, proved a source of much diversion to the native congregation, and poor Luisa was subjected to the usual Samoan jests about the *toe'ina* and *ulu tula* (old man and bald head), and would arrive from the church at her father's hell in a state of suppressed exasperation.

The happy marriage had been celebrated by Tom and his *clientèle* in a manner befitting the occasion and the supposed wealth of the bridegroom. Then none of us saw Luisa for a week at the bathing-place, and her non-appearance was discussed with interest at the nightly kava-drinking at half-caste Johnny Hall's public-house. Old Toi'foi, duenna of the kava-chewing girls, used to say solemnly that the old man had Luisa locked up in her room as she was *vale* (obstinate), and sat on a chair outside and looked at her through a hole in the wall.

· · · · ·

An hour after midnight on one of those silent tropic nights when naught is heard but the muffled boom of the ocean swell on the outer reef, a shot rang out through the sleeping village, and then a long wail as of some one in mortal agony or terror. Leger, the Canadian carpenter at Macfarlane's store, was, in company with Alvord the Swearer, and Pedro the Publican, and many of us general sinners, up late at the kava-bowl when Leva, the prettiest girl on the

Point, and the most notorious *nymphe du beach* in Apia (there are no pavements in Samoa), dashed in amongst us with the announcement that "Luisa was dead." In another ten seconds we kava-drinkers, with unsteady legs but clear heads, were outside on our way to Black Tom's house, which was within pistol-shot.

. . . . .

An old man with a throat cut from ear to ear is not a cheerful sight at any time, and we turned quickly away from where he lay on the once spotless white bed, now an ensanguined horror, to look at poor Luisa, who lay on a mat on the floor, gasping out her brief young life. Her head was pillowed on her mother's bosom, and down her side the blood ran from the jagged bullet-hole. On a chair sat the herculean figure of Black Tom with his face in his hands, through which splashed heavy tears. Slowly he rocked himself to and fro in the manner of his race when strongly moved; and when he tried to speak there only struck upon our ears a horrible gasping noise that somehow made us turn again to the awful thing on the bed to see if it had aught to say upon the matter.

. . . . .

Luisa spoke but little. The kind-faced, quiet-voiced missionary doctor told her that which she already knew too well; and then we drew away while he spoke of other things, and we saw the look of dread and horror on the comely young face pass away and a faint smile part the lips that were already touched by the grim shadow of coming dissolution. Some of her village playmates and companions, with wet cheeks, bent their faces and touched her lips with theirs, and to each she sighed a low *To Fa* of farewell, and then she looked toward the shaking bent figure in the chair and beckoned him over. With noiseless tread he came, and then, with her very soul looking at him from her great, death-stricken eyes, she murmured, "Fear not, my father, my mouth is covered by the hand of Death; farewell!"

 . . . . .

The sound of the soft lapping of the falling tide came through the open window as Luisa spoke again to Toĕ-o-le-Sasa, the Maid of Apia—" E Toe, *e pae afea te tai?*" *("*When is the tide out?*")* And the girl answered with a sob in her throat, "In quite a little while, O friend of my heart."

"*Ua lelei.* (It is well.) And as the waters run out so does my soul float away!" and she turned her face to her mother's bosom. And as we went softly out from the room and stood upon the path with the lofty palm-plumes rustling above us, we saw the first swirling wave of the incoming tide ripple round Matautu Point and plash on Hamilton's beach. And from within the silent house answered the wail of Death.

THE FALLACIES OF HILLIARD

The Fallacies of Hilliard.

WITH clenched hand grasping the two letters—the one that sank his last hope of saving his plantation, and the other that blasted his trust in human nature—Hilliard, the planter of Nairai Viwa, walked with quick, firm step to his house, and sat down to think awhile. The great cotton "burst-up" had ruined most men in Fiji, and although long delayed in his case the blow had crushed him utterly.

An angry flush tinged his set features for a few seconds as he re-read the curt, almost savage denial, by his father of the "couple of thousand" asked for. "A fool to resign his commission in the Service and go into a thing he knew nothing about, merely to humour the fantastic whim of a woman of fashion who will, no doubt, now sheer very clear of your wrecked fortunes."

Ten minutes previously when Hilliard, who had thought his father would never see him go under for the sake of a couple of thou., had read these lines he had smiled, even with the despair of broken fortune at his heart, as he looked at the other letter yet unopened.

Kitty, at least, would stick to him. He was not

a maudlin sentimentalist, but the memory of her farewell kisses was yet strong with him; and his past experiences of woman's weaknesses and his own strength justified him in thinking that in this one woman he had found his pearl of great price.

Then he read her letter; and as he read the tappa mallets at work in the Fijian houses hard by seemed to thump in unison with the dull beats of his heart as he stared at the correctly-worded and conventionally-expressed lines that mocked at his fond imaginings of but a few breaths back.

· · · · ·

Jimmy, the curly-headed half-caste who had brought him his letters from Levuka, had followed in his steps and was sitting, hat in hand, on the sofa before him when Hilliard raised his face. The fixed pallor had left his bronzed cheeks. For an instant the face of another man had passed before him—Lamington, his one-time fellow-officer, whom every one but Hilliard himself looked upon as being first "in the running" with the woman who had pledged herself to him. But, then, Lamington himself had told him that she had refused him, heir to a big fortune as he was, and they had shaken hands, and Lamington had wished him luck in his honest, good-natured fashion. "Perhaps," and here the dark flush mantled his forehead, "he's tried again and she's slung me. And I . . . what a damnably unpleasant and quick intuition of women's ways my old dad has! I always wondered why such a fiery devil as he was married such a milk-and-water creature as my good mother. By ——, I begin to think he went on safe lines, and I on a fallacy!"

· · · · ·

The stolid face of Jimmy recalled him to the present. He must give up the plantation and take a berth of some sort. From the sideboard he took a flask of liquor and poured out two big drinks.

"Here, Jimmy, my boy. This is the last drink you'll get on Nairai Viwa. I'm burst up, cleaned out, dead broke, and going to hell generally."

Jimmy grunted and held out his brown hand for the grog. "Yes? I s'pose you'll go to Levuka first? I'll give you a passage in the cutter."

Hilliard laughed with mingled bitterness and sarcasm. "Right, Jimmy. Levuka is much like the other place, and I'll get experience there, if I don't get a billet."

"Here's luck to you, sir, wherever you go," and Jimmy's thick lips glued themselves lovingly to the glass.

Hilliard drank his oft quietly, only muttering to himself, "Here's good-bye to the fallacies of hope," and then, being at bottom a man of sense and quick resolution, he packed his traps and at sunset went aboard the cutter. As they rippled along with the first puffs of the land-breeze, he glanced back but once at the lights of Nairai Viwa village that illumined the cutter's wake, and then, like a wise man, the hopes and dreams of the past drifted astern too.

And then for the next two years he drifted about from one group to another till he found an island that suited him well—no other white man lived there.

•   •   •   •   •

II.

The laughing, merry-voiced native children who, with speedy feet, ran to the house of Iliāti, the trader, to tell him that a visitor was coming from the man-of-war, had gathered with panting breath and hushed expectancy at the door as the figure of the naval officer turned a bend in the path, his right hand clasped with a proud air of proprietorship by that of the ten-year-old son of Alberti the Chief.

Iliāti, with a half-angry, half-pleased look, held out his hand.

"Lamington!"

"Hilliard! old fellow. Why didn't you come on board? Are all your old friends forgotten?"

. . . . .

"Pretty nearly, Lamington. Since I came a cropper over that accursed cotton swindle I've not had any inclination to meet any one I knew—especially any one in the Service, but"—and his voice rang honestly, "I always wondered whether you and I would ever meet again."

"Hilliard," and Lamington placed his hand on the trader's shoulder, "I know all about it. And look here, old man. I saw her only two months ago—at her especial request. She sent for me to talk about you."

"Ah!" and the trader's voice sounded coldly, "I thought, long ago, that she had reconsidered her foolish decision of other days and had long since become Mrs. Lamington. But it doesn't interest me, old fellow. Can you drink Fiji rum, Lamington? Haven't anything better to offer you."

"I'll drink anything you've got, old fellow, even liquid Tophet boiled down to a small half-pint; but I want you to listen to me first. I've been a bit of a scoundrel to you, but, by God, old man, I exchanged into the beastly old *Petrel* for this cruise expressly to find you and make a clean breast of it. I promised her I would."

"Confound it all, Lamington, don't harrow your feelings needlessly, and let us have the rum and talk about anything else."

"No, we won't. Look here, Hilliard, it sounds beastly low, but I must get it out. We met again—at a ball in Sydney more than two years ago. Some infernal chattering women were talking a lot of rot about the planters in Fiji having very pretty and privileged native servants—and all that, you know. She fired up and denied it, but came and asked me if it was true, and I was mean enough not to give it a straight denial. How the devil it happened I can't tell you, but we danced a deuce of a lot and I lost my senses and asked her again, and she said 'Yes.' Had she been any other woman but Miss ——, I would have concluded that the soft music and all that had dazed her. It does sometimes—lots of 'em; makes the most virtuous wife wish she could be a sinner and resume her normal goodness next day. But Kitty is different. And it was only that infernal twaddle caused it and made her write you that letter. A week hadn't passed before she wrote to me and told me how miserable she was. But I knew all through she didn't care a d—— about me. And that's the way it occurred, old man."

Hilliard's hand met his. "Say no more about it,

Lamington; it's a *mea matē*, as we say here—a thing that is past."

"But, good God, old fellow, you don't understand. She's written ever so many times to you. No one in Levuka knew where you had gone to; there's thousands of islands in the South Seas. And this letter here," he held it toward him, "she gave to me, and I promised her on my honour as a man to effect an exchange into the *Petrel* and find you."

"Thanks, Lamington. You always were a good fellow." He laid the letter on the table quietly and rose and got the rum.

. . . . .

A young native girl, with deep lustrous eyes shining from a face of almost childish innocence, had entered the door and stood with one bare and softly-rounded arm clasped round the neck of Alberti's little son. Her lips parted in a smile as Lamington, with a gasping cough, set down his glass after drinking the potent spirit, and she set her brows in mock ferocity at Hilliard who drank his down like an old-time beachcomber.

"By Jove, Hilliard, what an astonishingly pretty face! She could give any New Orleans creole points. Time you got out of this before some of the Rotumah beauties make you forget things; and oh, by the way, I'm forgetting things. Remember you are to come aboard and dine with us to-night, and that you're in indifferent health, and that Captain ——, of Her Majesty's ship *Petrel*, is going to give you a passage to Sydney."

At an angry sign from Hilliard the girl disappeared. Then he shook his head. "No, Lamington. I appreciate your kindness, but cannot accept it. I've been here two years now, and Alberti, the principal local chief, thinks no end of me; and he's a deuced fine fellow, and has been as good as ten fathers to me. And I've business matters to attend to as well."

. . . . .

Lamington pressed him no further. "Lucky devil," he thought. "I suppose he'll clear out in the trading schooner to Sydney, next week; be there long before us any way, and I'll find them well over the first stage of married infatuation when I see him next."

Another hour's chat of old times and old shipmates in the *Challenger*, and Lamington, with his honest, clean-shaven face looking into the quiet, impassive features of the ex-officer, had gripped his hand and gone, and Hilliard went over to the house of Alberti, the chief, to drink *kava*—and see the old French priest. From there, an hour afterward, he saw the cruiser with wet, shining sides dip into the long roll of the ocean swell, as with the smoke pouring from her yellow funnel she was lost to sight rounding the point.

. . . . .

Said the son of Alberti to Léla, the innocent-faced girl with the dancing, starlike eyes and red lips, as they stood watching the last curling rings of the steamer's smoke—"And so that is why I knew much of what the *papalagi* from the man-of-war said to your Iliāti; Alberti, my father, has taught me much of your man's tongue. And, look thou, Léla the Cunning, Iliāti hath a wife in his own country!"

"Pah!"—and she shook her long, wavy locks composedly, and then plucked a scarlet hibiscus flower

to stick in front of one of her pretty little ears—
"what does that matter to me, fathead? I am she
here; and when Iliāti goeth away to her she will be
me there. But he loveth me more than any other on
Rotumah, and hath told me that where he goeth I
shall go also. And who knoweth but that if I have a
son he may marry me? Then shalt thou see such a
wedding-feast as only rich people give. And listen—
for why should I not tell thee: 'Tis well to starve thyself now, for it may be to-morrow, for look! fathead,
there goeth the priest into thy father's house, and
Iliāti is already there."

A TALE OF A MASK

A Tale of a Mask.

LANNIGAN, who lived on Motukoe, was in debt to his firm. This was partly due to his fondness for trade gin and partly because Bully Hayes had called at the island a month or so back and the genial Bully and he had played a game or two of poker.

"I'll give you your revenge when I come back from the Carolines, Lannigan," said the redoubtable captain as he scooped in every dollar of the trader's takings for the past six months. And Lannigan, grasping his hand warmly and declaring it was a pleasure to be "claned out by a gintleman," bade him good-bye and went to sleep away from home for a day with some native friends. Tariro, his Manhiki wife, had a somewhat violent temper, and during the poker incident had indulged in much vituperative language outside, directed at white men in general and Lannigan in particular.

· · · · ·

"See, thou swiller of gin, see what thy folly has brought us to," said the justly-incensed Tariro, when he came back, and with her took stock of his trade goods; "a thousand and five hundred dollars' worth of trade came we here with, and thou hast naught to show for it but five casks of oil and a few stinking shark-fins; and surely the ship of the *malo* (his firm) will be here this month."

Lannigan was in a bit of a fix. The firm he was trading for on Motukoe didn't do business in the same free-and-easy way as did Bobby Towns' captains and the unconventional Bully Hayes. They made him sign papers, and every time the ship came the rufous-headed Scotch supercargo took stock, and a violent altercation would result over the price of the trade; but as the trader generally had a big lot of produce for the ship, matters always ended amicably. He—or rather his wife, Tariro—was too good a trader to have an open rupture with, and the wordy warfare always resulted in the trader saying, in his matter-of-fact way, "Well, I suppose it's right enough. You only rob me wanst in twelve months, and I rob the natives here every day of my life. Give me in a case of gin, an' I'll send ye a pig."

. . . . .

But he had never been so much in debt as he was now. Tariro and he talked it over, and hit upon a plan. He was to say, when the ship came, that he had but five casks of oil; all his trade had been sold for cash, and the cash—a thousand dollars—represented by a bag of copper bolts picked up on the reef from an old wreck, was to be taken off to the ship and accidentally dropped overboard as it was being passed up on deck. This was Lannigan's idea, and Tariro straightway tied up the bolts in readiness in many thicknesses of sail-cloth.

. . . . .

"Here's Lannigan coming," called out the captain

of the trading vessel to the supercargo, a week or so afterwards, "and that saucy Manhiki woman as usual with him, to see that he doesn't get drunk. The devil take such as her! There's no show of getting him tight."

"How are you, Lannigan?" said the supercargo, wiping his perspiring brow. He had just come out of the hold where he had been opening tinned meats, and putting all the "blown" tins he could find into one especial case—for Lannigan. This was what he called "makin' a mairgin for loss on the meats, which didna pay well."

"Fine," said the genial Lannigan, "an' I haven't got but five casks of oil for yez. Devil a drop av oil would the people make when they looked at the bewtiful lot av trade ye gave me last time. They just rushed me wid cash, an' I tuk a matter av a thousand dollars or so in a month."

"Verra guid business," said the supercargo, "but ye made a gran' meestake in selling the guids for Cheelian dollars instead of oil. An' sae I must debit ye wi' a loss of twenty-five par cent. on the money——"

"Chile dollars be damned!" said Lannigan; "all good American dollars — we've had about twenty whaleships here, buyin' pigs an' poultry an' pearl shell."

"Twenty-one ship!" said Tariro, blowing the smoke of her cigarette through her pretty little nose.

"Whaur's the money, onyway?" said the supercargo; "let's get to business, Lannigan. Eh, mon, I've some verra fine beef for ye."

"Get the bag up out of the boat, Tariro," said the

trader; "it's mighty frightened I was havin' so much money in the house at wanst, wid all them rowdy Yankee sailors from the whaleships ashore here."

* * * * *

There was a great crowd of natives on deck—over a hundred—and the mate was swearing violently at them for getting in his way. The schooner was a very small vessel, and Motukoe being her first place of call for cargo, she was in light trim, having only her trade and a little ballast on board.

"Send those natives away from the galley," he called out to the cook, who was giving some of the young women ship-biscuits in exchange for young cocoanuts; "can't you see the ship keeps flying up in the wind with all those people for'ard!"

* * * * *

Hekemanu, Lannigan's native "Man Jack," sat in the boat towing alongside, with the bag of "dollars" at his feet. He and all the boat's crew were in the secret. Lannigan owned their souls; besides, they all liked him on Motukoe.

Tariro stood for a moment beside the captain, indulging in the usual broad "chaff," and then leaning over the rail she called out to Hekemanu: *Ta mai te taga tupe* ("give me the bag of money").

The man for'ard hauled on the line to bring the boat alongside the schooner, and Hekemanu stood up with the heavy bag in his hand.

"Hold on there, you fool! If you drop that bag I'll knock your head off," said the skipper. "Here, Mr. Bates, just you jump down and take that money from that native, or he'll drop it, sure."

Before Hekemanu had time to let it fall over the side the mate had jumped into the boat and taken it.

Lannigan, putting his head up out of the little cabin, groaned inwardly as he saw the mate step over the rail with the fateful bag and hand it to the supercargo.

"Be the powers, ye're in a mighty hurry for the money," said Lannigan, roughly, taking it from him, "ye might ax me if I had a mouth on me first."

The supercargo laughed and put a bottle of gin on the table, and Lannigan's fertile brain commenced to work. If he could only get the supercargo out of the cabin for a minute he meant to pick up the bag, and declaring he was insulted get it back into his boat and tell him to come and count it ashore. Then he could get capsized on the reef and lose it. They were always having "barneys," and it would only be looked upon as one of his usual freaks.

. . . . .

"What the deuce is that?" he said, pointing to a hideous, highly-coloured paper mask that hung up in the cabin.

The supercargo handed it to him. "It's for a man in Samoa—a silly, joking body, always playing pranks wi' the natives, and I thoct he would like the thing."

"Bedad, 'tis enough to scare the sowl out av the divil," said Lannigan.

Just then a mob of natives came aft, and the two men in the cabin heard the captain tell them to clear out again. They were saucy and wouldn't go. Hekemanu had told them of the failure of Lannigan's dodge, and they had an idea that the ship would take him away, and stood by to rescue him at the word of command.

"I'll verra soon hunt them," said the supercargo, with a proud smile, and he put the mask on his face. Tariro made a bolt on deck and called out to the natives that the supercargo was going to frighten them with a mask.

· · · · ·

Instead of wild yells of fear and jumping overboard, as he imagined would happen, the natives merely laughed, but edged away for'ard.

The schooner was in quite close to the reef; the water was very deep, and there was no danger of striking. She was under jib and mainsail only, but the breeze was fresh and she was travelling at a great rate. The wind being right off the land the skipper was hugging the reef as closely as possible, so as to bring up and anchor on a five-fathom patch about a mile away.

"Here, quit that fooling," he called out to the supercargo, "and come aft, you fellows! The ship is that much down by the head she won't pay off, with the helm hard up."

One look at the crowd of natives and another at the shore, and a wild idea came into Lannigan's head. He whispered to Tariro, who went up for'ard and said something to the natives. In another ten seconds some of them began to clamber out on the jib-boom, the rest after them.

"Come back!" yelled the skipper, jamming the helm hard up, as the schooner flew up into the wind. "Leggo peak halyards. By G—d! we are running ashore. Leggo throat halyards, too!"

A Tale of a Mask.

The mate flew to the halyards, and let go first the peak and then the throat halyards, but it was too late, and, with a swarm of natives packed together for'ard from the galley to the end of the jib-boom, she stuck her nose down, and, with stern high out of the water, like a duck chasing flies, she crashed into the reef—ran ashore dead to windward.

· · · · ·

No one was drowned. The natives took good care of the captain, mate, and supercargo, and helped them to save all they could. But Lannigan had a heavy loss—the bag of copper bolts had gone to the bottom.

THE COOK OF THE "SPREETOO SANTOO"

The Cook of the "*Spreetoo Santoo.*"

A STUDY IN BEACHCOMBERS.

WE were in Kitti Harbour, at Ponape, in the Carolines, when, at breakfast, a bleary-eyed, undersized, more-or-less-white man in a dirty pink shirt and dungaree pants, came below, and, slinging his filthy old hat over to the transoms, shoved himself into a seat between the mate and Jim Garstang, the trader.

"Mornin', captin," said he, without looking at the skipper, and helping himself to about two pounds of curry.

"Morning to you. Who the deuce are you, anyway? Are you the old bummer they call 'Espiritu Santo'?" said Garstang.

"That's me. I'm the man. But I ain't no bummer, don't you b'lieve it. I wos tradin' round here in these (lurid) islands afore you coves knowed where Ponape was."

"Are you the skunk that Wardell kicked off the Shenandoah for stealing a bottle of wine?" said the mate.

"That's me. There was goin' ter be trouble over that on'y that the Shennydor got properly well sunk by the *Allybarmer* (history wasn't his forte), and that

—— Wardell got d——d well drownded. Hingland haint a-goin' to let no Yankee insult nobody for nuthin'—an' I'm a blessed Englishman. I didn't steal the wine. Yer see, Wardell arst me off to dinner, and then we gets talkin' about polertics, an' I tells 'im 'e wos a lyin' pirut. Then he started foolin' around my woman, an' I up with a bottle of wine an'——"

"Why, you thundering liar," said Garstang, "you stole it out of the ward-room."

"I wouldn't call no man a liar if I was you, Mister —by G——, that Chinaman cook knows how to make curry."

He ate like a starving shark, and between mouthfuls kept up a running fire of lies and blasphemy. When he had eaten three platefuls of curry and drunk enough coffee to scald a pig, the skipper, who was gettin' tired of him, asked him if he had had enough.

Yes, he had had enough breakfast to last him a whole (Australian adjective) week.

"Then clear out on deck and swab the curry off your face, you beast!"

"That's always the way with you tradin' skippers. A stranger don't get no civility unless he comes aboard in a (red-painted) gig with a (crimson) umbrella and a (gory) 'elmet 'at, like a (vermilion) Consul."

The mate seized him, and, running him up the companion way, slung him out on deck.

. . . . .

"What do you think of him?" asked the skipper, a man fond of a joke—it was Bully Hayes. "I thought I'd let you all make his acquaintance. He's been bumming around the Ladrones and Pelews since

'50; used to be cook on a Manilla trading brig, the *Espiritu Santo*."

Then he told us how this wandering mass of blasphemy got his name of "Spreetoo Santoo." While in the brig he had been caught smuggling at Guam by the guarda costas, and had spent a year or two in the old prison fort at San Juan de 'Apra. (I don't know how he got out: perhaps his inherently alcoholic breath and lurid blasphemy made the old brick wall tumble down.)

After that he was always welcome in sailors' fo'c's'les by reason of his smuggling story, which would commence with—"When I was cook on the *Espiritu Santo*" (only he used the English instead of the Spanish name) "I got jugged by the gory gardy costers," &c., &c.

· · · · ·

When we came on deck he was sitting on the main-hatch with the Chinese carpenter—whose pipe he was smoking—and telling him that he ought to get rid of his native wife, who was a Gilbert Island girl, and buy a Ponape girl.

"I can git yer the pick o' the (crimson) island, an' it won't cost yer more'n a few (unprintable) dollars. I'm a (bad word) big man 'ere among the (adjective) natives."

Hung looked up at him stolidly with half-closed eyes. Then he took the pipe out of his mouth and said in a deadly cold voice—

"You palally liar, Spleetoo."

· · · · ·

He slouched aft again presently, and asked the mate,

in an amiable tone of voice, if he had "any (ruddy) noospapers from Sydney."

"What the devil do *you* want newspapers for?" inquired Hayes, turning round suddenly in his deck-chair, "you can't read, Spreetoo."

"Can't read, eh?" and his red-rimmed, lashless eyes simulated intense indignation. "Wot about that 'ere (red) bishop at Manilla, as wanted me to chuck up me (scarlet) billet on the *Spreetoo Santoo* and travel through the (carnaged) Carryline Grewp as 's (sanguinary) sekketerry? 'Cos why? 'Cos there ain't any (blank) man atween 'ere an' 'ell as can talk the warious lingoes like me."

"Here," said the mate, giving him two or three old Maoriland newspapers—"here's some Auckland papers. Know anybody there?"

"No," he answered, promptly, "not a soul, but he knowed Sydney well. Larst time I wos there I sold old Bobby Towns £6,000 worth of oil—a bloomin' shipful. I got drunk, an' a (blank) policeman went through me in the cell and took the whole blessed lot outer me (scarlet) pocket." (Nine bad words omitted.)

"Bank notes?" queried Bully.

"No, sov'reigns—(gory) sov'reigns."

. . . . .

He asked us if we had seen any men-o'-war about lately, and said that the captain of H.M.S. —— had wanted to marry his daughter, but he wouldn't let her marry no man-o'-war cove after the way that —— Wardell had treated him. He thought he would go back to Sydney again for a spell. His brother had a flaming fine billet there.

"What is he?" asked Hayes.

"'E's a (blessed) Soopreme Court Judge, wears a (gory) wig big enough to make chafin' gear for a (crimson) fleet o' ships; 'e lives at Guvment 'Ouse, and 'e's rollin' in money an' drinks like a (carmine) fish. I thought I might see somethin' about the —— in a (blank) Sydney noospaper. I'll come in for all his (ensanguined) money when 'e dies."

Bully gave him a bottle of gin after a while. Then he hurriedly bade us farewell and went ashore.

LUPTON'S GUEST: A MEMORY OF THE EASTERN PACIFIC

Lupton's Guest: a Memory of the Eastern Pacific.

A LONG sweeping curve of coast, fringed with tall plumed palms casting wavering shadows on the yellow sand as they sway and swish softly to the breath of the brave trade-wind that whistles through the thickly-verdured hummocks on the weather side of the island, to die away into a soft breath as, after passing through the belt of cocoanuts, it faintly ripples the transparent depths of the lagoon—a broad sheet of blue and silver stretching away from the far distant western line of reef to the smooth, yellow beach at the foot of the palms on the easternmost islet. And here, beneath their lofty crowns, are the brown thatched huts of the people and the home of Lupton the trader.

. . . . .

This is Mururea. And, if it be possible, Mururea surpasses in beauty any other of the "cloud of islands" which, lying on the blue bosom of the Eastern Pacific like the islands of a dream, are called by their people the Paumotu. And these people—it is not of very long ago I speak—are a people unto themselves. Shy and suspicious of strangers, white or brown, and endued with that quick instinct of fear which impels untutored minds to slay, and which we, in our civilised ignorance, call savage treachery, they are yet kind-hearted and hospitable to those who learn their ways and regard their customs. A tall, light-skinned, muscular people, the men with long, straight, black hair, coiled up in a knot at the back, and the women—the descendants of those who sailed with broken Fletcher Christian and his comrades of the *Bounty* in quest of a place where to die—soft-voiced, and with big, timorous eyes.

. . . . .

'Twas here that Ben Peese, the handsome, savagely humorous, and voluble colleague of Captain " Bully " Hayes, the modern rover of the South Seas, one day appeared. Lupton, with his son and two natives, were out searching the beach of a little islet for turtles' eggs, when the boy, who had been sent to obtain a few young drinking cocoanuts from a tree some little distance away, called out, " *Te Pahi!* " (a ship). A few minutes passed, and then, outlined against the narrow strip of cocoanuts that grew on the north end of the main islet of the lagoon, Lupton saw the sails of a schooner making for the only opening—a narrow passage on the eastern side.

Now vessels came but rarely to Mururea, for Du Petit Thouars, the French Admiral of the Pacific fleet, had long since closed the group to the Sydney trading ships that once came there for pearl-shell, and Lupton felt uneasy. The vessel belonging to the Tahitian firm for whom he traded was not due for many months. Could the stranger be that wandering Ishmael of the sea—Peese? Only he—or his equally daring and dreaded colleague, Bully Hayes—would dare to sail a vessel of any size in among the coral "mushrooms" that studded the current-swept waters of the dangerous passage.

What did he want? And honest Frank Lupton, a quiet and industrious trader, thought of his store of pearl-shell and felt still more doubtful. And he knew Peese so well, the dapper, handsome little Englishman with the pleasant voice that had in it always a ripple of laughter—the voice and laugh that concealed his tigerish heart and savage vindictiveness. Lupton had children too—sons and daughters—and Peese, who looked upon women as mere articles of merchandise, would have thought no more of carrying off the trader's two pretty daughters than he would of "taking" a cask of oil or a basket of pearl-shell.

· · · · ·

His anxious face, paling beneath the tropic bronze of twenty years' ocean wanderings, betrayed his feelings to the two natives who were now pulling the boat with all their strength to gain the village, and one—Maora, his wife's brother, a big, light-skinned man, with that keen, hawk-like visage peculiar to the people of the eastern islands of Polynesia, said—

"'Tis an evil day, Farani! No ship but that of the Little Man with the Beard hath ever passed into the lagoon since the great English fighting ship came inside" (he spoke of 1863), "for the reef hath grown and spread out and nearly closed it. Only the Little Bearded Devil would dare it, for he hath been here twice with the Man of the Strong Hand" (Hayes). "And, Farani, listen! 'The hand to the club!'"

They ceased pulling. From the village came the

sound of an almost forgotten cry—a signal of danger to the dwellers under the palms—" The hand to the club!"—meaning for the men to arm.

* * * * *

Lupton hesitated. The natives would, he knew, stand to him to a man if violence to or robbery of him were attempted. But to gain the village he must needs pass close the vessel, and to pass on and not board her would savour of cowardice—and Lupton was an Englishman, and his twenty years' wanderings among the dangerous people of some of the islands of the Paumotu Group had steeled his nerves to meet any danger or emergency. So, without altering the course of the boat, he ran alongside of the vessel— which was a brigantine—just as she was bringing to, and looking up, he saw the face he expected.

"How are you, Lupton, my dear fellow?" said Peese, as the trader gained the deck, wringing his hand effusively, as if he were a long-lost brother. "By Heavens! I'm glad to meet a countryman again, and that countryman Frank Lupton. Don't like letting your hand go." And still grasping the trader's rough hand in his, delicate and smooth as a woman's, he beamed upon him with an air of infantile pleasure.

* * * * *

This was one of Peese's peculiarities—an affectation of absolute affection for any Englishman he met, from the captain of a man-of-war (these, however, he avoided as much as possible), to a poor beachcomber with but a grass girdle round his loins.

"What brings you here, Captain Peese?" said

Lupton, bluntly, as his eye sought the village, and saw the half-naked figures of his native following leaving his house in pairs, each carrying between them a square box, and disappearing into the *puka* scrub. It was his pearl-shell. Màmeri, his wife, had scented danger, and the shell at least was safe, however it befell. Peese's glance followed his, and the handsome little captain laughed, and slapped the gloomy-faced and suspicious trader on the back with an air of *camaraderie*.

"My dear fellow, what an excessively suspicious woman your good Màmeri is! But do not be alarmed. I have not come here to do any business this time, but to land a passenger, and as soon as his traps are on the beach I'm off again to Maga Reva. Such are the exigencies, my dear Lupton, of a trading captain's life in the South Seas, I cannot even spare the time to go on shore with you and enjoy the hospitality of the good Màmeri and your two fair daughters. But come below with me and see my passenger." And he led the way to his cabin.

 . . . .

The passenger's appearance, so Lupton told me, "was enough to make a man's blood curdle," so ghastly pale and emaciated was he. He rose as Lupton entered and extended his hand.

"My friend here," said the worthy little Ishmael, bowing and caressing his long silky beard, "is, ah, hum, Mr. Brown. He is, as you will observe, my dear Lupton, in a somewhat weak state of health, and is in search of some retired spot where he may recuperate sufficiently——"

"Don't lie unnecessarily, sir."

Peese bowed affably and smiled, and the stranger addressed Lupton.

"My name is not Brown—'tis of no consequence what it is; but I am, indeed, as you see, in a bad way, with but a few months at most to live. Captain Peese, at my request, put into this lagoon. He has told me that the place is seldom visited by ships, and that the people do not care about strangers. Yet, have you, Mr. Lupton, any objections to my coming ashore here, and living out the rest of my life? I have trade goods sufficient for all requirements, and will in no way interfere with or become a charge upon you."

Lupton considered. His influence with the people of Mururea was such that he could easily overcome their objections to another white man landing; but he had lived so long apart from all white associations that he did not care about having the even monotony of his life disturbed. And then, he thought, it might be some queer game concocted between the sick man and the chattering little sea-hawk that sat beside him stroking and fondling his flowing beard. He was about to refuse when the sunken, eager eyes of "Mr. Brown" met his in an almost appealing look that disarmed him of all further suspicion.

"Very well, sir. The island is as free to you as to me. But, still, I *could* stop any one else from living here if I wished to do so. But you do look very ill, no mistake about that. And, then, you ain't going to trade against me! And I suppose you'll pass me your word that there isn't any dodge between you and the captain here to bone my shell and clear out?"

For answer the sick man opened a despatch-box that lay on the cabin table, and took from it a bag of money.

*   *   *   *

"This," he said, "is the sum I agreed to pay Captain Peese to land me on any island of my choice in the Paumotu Archipelago, and this unsigned order here is in his favour on the Maison Brander of Tahiti for a similar sum."

Signing the paper he pushed it with the money over to Peese, and then went on :—

"I assure you, Mr. Lupton, that this is the only transaction I have ever had with Captain Peese. I came to him in Tahiti, hearing he was bound to the Paumotu Group. I had never heard of him before, and after to-day I will not, in all human probability, see him again."

"Perfectly correct, my dear sir," said Peese. "And now, as our business is finished, perhaps our dear friend, Lupton, will save me the trouble of lowering a boat by taking you ashore in his own, which is alongside."

Five minutes later and Lupton and the stranger were seated in the boat.

"Good-bye, my dear Lupton, and *adios* my dear Mr. Brown. I shall ever remember our pleasant relations on board my humble little trading vessel," cried the renowned Peese, who, from former associations, had a way of drifting into the Spanish tongue—and prisons and fetters—which latter he once wore for many a weary day on the cruiser *Hernandez Pizarro* on his way to the gloomy prison of Manilla.

The boat had barely traversed half the distance to

the shore ere the brigantine's anchor was hove-up and at her bows, and then Peese, with his usual cool assurance, beat her through the intricate passage and stood out into the long roll of the Pacific.

. . . . .

When Lupton, with his "walking bone bag," as he mentally called the stranger, entered his house, Màmeri, his bulky native wife, uttered an exclamation of pity, and placing a chair before him uttered the simple word of welcome *Iorana!* and the daughters, with wonder-lit star-like eyes, knelt beside their father's chair and whispered, "Who is he, Farani?"

And Lupton could only answer, "I don't know, and won't ask. Look to him well."

He never did ask. One afternoon nearly a year afterwards, as Lupton and Trenton, the supercargo of the *Marama*, sat on an old native *marae* at Arupahi, the Village of Four Houses, he told the strange story of his sick guest.

. . . . .

The stranger had at first wished to have a house built for himself, but Lupton's quiet place and the shy and reserved natures of his children made him change his intention and ask Lupton for a part of his house. It was given freely—where are there more generous-hearted men than these world-forgotten, isolated traders?—and here the Silent Man, as the people of Mururea called him, lived out the few months of his life. That last deceptive stage of his insidious disease had given him a fictitious strength. On many occasions, accompanied by the trader's children, he would walk to the north point of the low-lying island, where the cloudy spume of the surge was thickest and where the hollow and resonant crust of the black reef was perforated with countless air-holes, through which the water hissed and roared, and shot high in air, to fall again in misty spray.

And here, with dreamy eyes, he would sit under the shade of a clump of young cocoanuts, and watch the boil and tumble of the surf, whilst the children played with and chased each other about the clinking sand. Sometimes he would call them to him—Farani the boy, and Teremai and Lorani, the sweet-voiced and tender-eyed girls—and ask them to sing to him; and in their soft semi-Tahitian dialect they would sing the old songs that echoed in the ears of the desperate men of the *Bounty* that fatal dawn when, with bare-headed, defiant Bligh drifting astern in his boat, they headed back for Tahiti and death.

.   .   .   .   .

Four months had passed when one day the strange white man, with Lupton's children, returned to the village. As they passed in through the doorway with some merry chant upon their lips, they saw a native seated on the matted floor. He was a young man, with straight, handsome features, such as one may see any day in Eastern Polynesia, but the children, with terrified faces, shrank aside as they passed him and went to their father.

The pale face of the Silent Man turned inquiringly to Lupton, who smiled.

"'Tis Màmeri's teaching, you know. She is a Catholic from Màgareva, and prays and tells her beads enough to work a whaleship's crew into heaven. But this man is a 'Soul Catcher,' and if any one of us here got sick, Màmeri would let the faith she was reared in go to the wall and send for the 'Soul Catcher.' He's a kind of an all-round prophet, wizard, and general wisdom merchant. Took over the soul-catching business from his father—runs in the family, you know."

"Ah!" said the Silent Man in his low, languid tones, looking at the native, who, the moment he had entered, had bent his eyes to the ground, "and in which of his manifold capacities has he come to see you, Lupton?"

Lupton hesitated a moment, then laughed.

"Well, sir, he says he wants to speak to you. Wants to *pahihi* (talk rot), I suppose. It's his trade, you know. I'd sling him out only that he isn't a bad sort of a fellow—and a bit mad—and Màmeri says he'll quit as soon as he has had his say."

"Let him talk," said the calm, quiet voice; "I like these people, and like to hear them talk—better than I would most white men."

. . . . . .

Then, with his dark, dilated eyes moving from the pale face of the white man to that of Lupton, the native wizard and Seer of Unseen Things spoke. Then again his eyes sought the ground.

"What does he say?" queried Lupton's guest.

"D—— rot," replied the trader, angrily.

"Tell me exactly, if you please. I feel interested."

"Well, he says that he was asleep in his house when his 'spirit voice' awoke him and said "—here Lupton paused and looked at his guest, and then, seeing the faint smile of amused interest on his melancholy features, resumed, in his rough, jocular way—"and said—the 'spirit voice,' you know—that your soul was struggling to get loose, and is going away from you to-night. And the long and short of it is that this young fellow here wants to know if you'll let him save it—keep you from dying, you know. Says he'll do the job for nothing, because you're a good man, and a friend to all the people of Mururea."

"Mr. Brown" put his thin hand across his mouth, and his eyes smiled at Lupton. Then some sudden, violent emotion stirred him, and he spoke with such quick and bitter energy that Lupton half rose from his seat in vague alarm.

"Tell him," he said—"that is, if the language expresses it—that my soul has been in hell these ten years, and its place filled with ruined hopes and black despair," and then he sank back on his couch of mats, and turned his face to the wall.

The Seer of Unseen Things, at a sign from the now angry Lupton, rose to his feet. As he passed the trader he whispered—

"Be not angry with me, Farani; art not thou and all thy house dear to me, the Snarer of Souls and Keeper Away of Evil Things? And I can truly make a snare to save the soul of the Silent Man, if he so wishes it." The low, impassioned tones of the wizard's voice showed him to be under strong emotion, and Lupton, with smoothened brow, placed his hand on the native's chest in token of amity.

"Farani," said the wizard, "see'st thou these?" and he pointed to where, in the open doorway, two large white butterflies hovered and fluttered. They were a species but rarely seen in Mururea, and the natives had many curious superstitions regarding them.

"Aye," said the trader, "what of them?"

"Lo, they are the spirits that await the soul of him

who sitteth in thy house. One is the soul of a woman, the other of a man; and their bodies are long ago dust in a far-off land. See, Farani, they hover and wait, wait, wait. To-morrow they will be gone, but then another may be with them."

Stopping at the doorway the tall native turned, and again his strange, full black eyes fixed upon the figure of Lupton's guest. Then slowly he untied from a circlet of polished pieces of pearl-shell strung together round his sinewy neck a little round leaf-wrapped bundle. And with quiet assured step he came and stood before the strange white man and extended his hand.

"Take it, O man, with the swift hand and the strong heart, for it is thine."

And then he passed slowly out.

Lupton could only see that as the outside wrappings of *fala* leaves fell off they revealed a black substance, when Mr. Brown quickly placed it in the bosom of his shirt.

. . . . .

"And sure enough," continued Lupton, knocking the ashes from his pipe out upon the crumbling stones of the old marae, and speaking in, for him, strangely softened tones, "the poor chap did die that night, leastways at *kalaga moa* (cockcrow), and then he refilled his pipe in silence, gazing the while away out to the North-West Point."

. . . . .

"What a curious story!" began the supercargo, after an interval of some minutes, when he saw that Lupton, usually one of the merriest-hearted wanderers that rove to and fro in Polynesia, seemed strangely silent and affected, and had turned his face from him.

He waited in silence till the trader chose to speak again.

Away to the westward, made purple by the sunset haze of the tropics, lay the ever-hovering spume-cloud of the reef of North-West Point—the loved haunt of Lupton's guest—and the muffled boom of the ceaseless surf deepened now and then as some mighty roller tumbled and crashed upon the flat ledges of blackened reef.

· · · · ·

At last the trader turned again to the supercargo, almost restored to his usual equanimity. "I'm a pretty rough case, Mr. ——, and not much given to any kind of sentiment or squirming, but I would give half I'm worth to have him back again. He sort of got a pull on my feelin's the first time he ever spoke to me, and as the days went on, I took to him that much that if he'd a wanted to marry my little Teremai I'd have given her to him cheerful. Not that we ever done much talkin', but he'd sit night after night and make me talk, and when I'd spun a good hour's yarn he'd only say, 'Thank you, Lupton, good-night,' and give a smile all round to us, from old Màmeri to the youngest *tama*, and go to bed. And yet he did a thing that'll go hard agin' him, I fear."

"Ah," said Trenton, "and so he told you at the last—I mean his reason for coming to die at Mururea."

"No, he didn't. He only told me something; Peese told me the rest. And he laughed when he told me," and the dark-faced trader struck his hand on his knee. "Peese would laugh if he saw his mother crucified."

"Was Peese back here again, then?" inquired Trenton.

"Yes, two months ago. He hove-to outside, and came ashore in a canoe. Said he wanted to hear how his dear friend Brown was. He only stayed an hour, and then cleared out again."

"Did he die suddenly?" the supercargo asked, his mind still bent on Lupton's strange visitor.

"No. Just before daylight he called me to him—with my boy. He took the boy's hand and said he'd have been glad to have lived after all. He had been happy in a way with me and the children here in Mururea. Then he asked to see Teremai and Lorani. They both cried when they saw he was a goin'—all native-blooded people do that if they cares anything at all about a white man, and sees him dyin'."

"Have you any message, or anything to say in writin', sir?" I says to him.

He didn't answer at once, only took the girls' hands in his, and kisses each of 'em on the face, then he says, "No, Lupton, neither. But send the children away now. I want you to stay with me to the last—which will be soon."

Then he put his hand under his pillow, and took out a tiny little parcel, and held it in his closed hand.

. . . . .

"Mr. Lupton, I ask you before God to speak honestly. Have you, or have you not, ever heard of me, and why I came here to die, away from the eyes of men?"

"No, sir," I said. "Before God I know no more of you now than the day I first saw you."

"Can you, then, tell me if the native soul-doctor

who came here last night is a friend of Captain Peese? Did he see Peese when I landed here? Has he talked with him?"

"No. When you came here with Peese, the soul-seer was away at another island. And as for talking with him, how could he? Peese can't speak two words of Paumotu."

He closed his eyes a minute. Then he reached out his hand to me and said, "Look at that; what is it?"

It was the little black thing that the Man Who Sees Beyond gave him, and was a curious affair altogether. "You know what an *aitu taliga* is?" asked Lupton.

"Yes; a 'devil's ear'—that's what the natives call fungus."

. . . . .

"Well," continued Lupton, "this was a piece of dried fungus, and yet it wasn't a piece of fungus. It was the exact shape of a human heart—just as I've seen a model of it made of wax. That hadn't been its natural shape, but the sides had been brought together and stitched with human hair—by the soul-doctor, of course. I looked at it curiously enough, and gave it back to him. His fingers closed round it again."

"What is it?" he says again.

"It's a model of a human heart," says I, "made of fungus."

"My God!" he says, "how could he know?" Then he didn't say any more, and in another half-hour or so he dies, quiet and gentlemanly like. I looked for the heart with Màmeri in the morning—it was gone.

. . . . .

"Well, we buried him. And now look here, Mr. ——, as sure as I believe there's a God over us, I believe that that native soul-catcher *has* dealings with the Devil. I had just stowed the poor chap in his coffin and was going to nail it down when the kanaka wizard came in, walks up to me, and says he wants to see the dead man's hand. Just to humour him I lifted off the sheet. The soul-catcher lifted the dead man's hands carefully, and then I'm d——d if he didn't lay that dried heart on his chest and press the hands down over it."

"What's that for?" says I.

"'Tis the heart of the woman he slew in her sleep. Let it lie with him, so that there may be peace between them at last," and then he glides away without another word.

. . . . .

"I let it stay, not thinking much of it at the time. Well, as I was tellin' you, Peese came again. Seeing that I had all my people armed, I treated him well and we had a chat, and then I told him all about 'Mr. Brown's' death and the soul-saver and the dried heart. And then Peese laughs and gives me this newspaper cutting. I brought it with me to show you."

Trenton took the piece of paper and read.

. . . . .

"'Lester Mornington made his escape from the State prison at San Quentin (Cal.) last week, and is stated to be now on his way either to Honolulu or Tahiti. It has been ascertained that a vast sum of money has been disbursed in a very systematic manner during the last few weeks to effect his release. Although nearly eight years have elapsed since he committed his terrible crime, the atrocious nature of it will long be remembered. Young, wealthy, respected, and talented, he had been married but half a year when the whole of the Pacific Slope was startled with the intelligence that he had murdered his beautiful young wife, who had, he found, been disloyal to him.

"'Entering the bedroom he shot his sleeping wife through the temples, and then with a keen-edged knife had cut out her still-beating heart. This, enclosed in a small box, he took to the house of the man who had wronged him, and desired him to open it and look at the contents. He did so, and Mornington, barely giving him time to realise the tragedy, and that his perfidy was known, shot him twice, the wounds proving fatal next day. The murderer made good his escape to Mexico, only returning to California a month ago, when he was recognised (although disguised) and captured, and at the time of his escape was within two days of the time of his trial before Judge Crittenden.'"

. . . . .

"There's always a woman in these things," said Lupton, as the supercargo gave him back the slip. "Come on."

And he got down from his seat on the wall. "There's Màmeri calling us to *kaikai*—stewed pigeons. She's a bully old cook; worth her weight in Chile dollars."

IN NOUMÉA

In Nouméa.

CHESTER was listening to those charming musicians, the convict band, playing in Nouméa, and saw in the crowd a man he knew—more, an old friend, S——. The recognition was mutual and pleasing to both. They had not met for six years. He was then chief officer of a China steamer; now he was captain of a big tramp steamer that had called in to load nickel ore. "Who," exclaimed Chester, "would ever have thought of meeting *you* here?"

He laughed and replied: "I came with a purpose. You remember Miss ——, to whom I was engaged in Sydney?"

Chester nodded, expecting from the sparkle in S——'s dark brown eye that he was going to hear a little gush about her many wifely qualities.

"Well, I was in Sydney three times after I saw you. We were to be married as soon as I got a command. Two years ago I was there last. She had got married. Wrote me a letter saying she knew my calmer judgment would finally triumph over my anger—she had accepted a good offer, and although I might be nettled, perhaps, at first, yet she was sure my good sense would applaud her decision in marrying a man who, although she could never love him as she loved me, was very rich. But she would always look forward to meeting me again. That was all."

"Hard lines," said Chester.

"My dear boy, I thought that at first, when her letter knocked me flat aback. But I got over it, and I swore I would pay her out. And I came to this den of convicts to do it, and I did it—yesterday. She is here."

"*Here?*" said Chester.

And then he learnt the rest of Captain S——'s story. A year after his lady-love had jilted him he received a letter from her in England. She was in sad trouble, she said. Her husband, a Victorian official, was serving five years for embezzlement. Her letter was suggestive of a desire to hasten to the "protection" of her sailor lover. She wished, she said, that her husband were dead. But dead or alive she would always hate *him*.

S—— merely acknowledged her letter and sent her £25. In another six months he got a letter from Fiji. She was a governess there, she said, at £75 a year. Much contrition and love, also, in this letter. S—— sent another £25, and remarked that he would see her soon. Fate one day sent him to take command of a steamer in Calcutta bound to Fiji with coolies, thence to Nouméa to load nickel ore. And all the way out across the tropics S——'s heart was leaping at the thought of seeing his lost love— and telling her that he hated her for her black frozen treachery.

As soon as he had landed his coolies he cautiously

set about discovering the family with whom she lived. No one could help him, but a planter explained matters: "I know the lady for whom you inquire, but she doesn't go by that name. Ask any one about Miss ——, the barmaid. She has gone to New Caledonia."

He asked, and learned that she was well known; and S—— wondered why she had brought her beauty to such a climate as that of Fiji when it would have paid her so much better to parade it in Melbourne.

The evening of the day on which his steamer arrived at Nouméa a man brought him a letter. He showed it to Chester.

MY DARLING WILL,—Thank God you have come, for surely you have come for me—my heart tells me so. For God's sake wait on board for me. I will come at eight. To live in this place is breaking my heart. Ever yours,——

She came. He stood her kisses passively, but gave none in return, until she asked him to kiss her. "When you are my wife," he said, evasively. And then—she must have loved him—she burst out into passionate sobs and fell at his feet in the quiet cabin and told him of her debased life in Fiji. "But, as God hears me, Will, that is all past since your last letter. I was mad. I loved money and did not care how I got it. I left Fiji to come here, intending to return to Australia. But, Will, dear Will, if it is only to throw me overboard, take me away from this hell upon earth. For your sake, Will, I have resisted them here, although I suffer daily, hourly, torture and insult. I have no money, and I am afraid to die and end my sufferings."

Captain S——, speaking calmly and slowly, placed money in her hand and said, "You must not see me again till the day I am ready for sea. Then bring your luggage and come on board."

With a smothered sob bursting from her, despite the joy in her heart, the woman turned and left him. Then S—— went up to the Café Palais and played billiards with a steady hand.

· · · · ·

There was a great number of people on board to see Captain S—— away. Presently a boat came alongside, and a young lady with sweet red lips and shiny hair ascended to the deck.

"Hèlas!" said a French officer to S——, "and so you are taking away the fair one who won't look at us poor exiles of Nouvelle."

With a timid smile and fast-beating heart the woman gained the quarter-deck. In front of her stood the broad-shouldered, well-groomed Captain S——, cold, impassive, and deadly pale, with a cruel joy in his breast.

The woman stood still. There was something so appalling in that set white face before her, that her slight frame quivered with an unknown dread. And then the captain spoke, in slow, measured words that cut her to her inmost soul.

"Madam, I do not take passengers!"

No answer. Only short, gasping breaths as she steadied her hand on the rail.

And then, turning to one of the Frenchmen: "M. ——, will you request this—this lady to go on shore? She is known to me as a woman of infamous reputation in Fiji. I cannot for a moment entertain the idea of having such a person on board my ship."

Before the shuddering creature fell a man caught her, and then she was placed in the boat and taken ashore. Of course some of the Frenchmen thought it right to demand an explanation from S——, who said—

"I've none to give, gentlemen. If any of you want to fight me, well and good, although I don't like quarrelling over a pavement-woman. Besides, I rather think you'll find that the lady will *now* be quite an acquisition to you."

But S——'s revenge was not complete. He had previously arranged matters with his engineer, who presently came along and announced an accident to the machinery—the steamer would be delayed a couple of days. He wanted to see her again—so he told Chester.

"It was a cruel thing," said his friend.

"Bah!" said S——, "come with me."

In the crowded bar of the café a woman was laughing and talking gaily. Something made her look up. She put her hand to her eyes and walked slowly from the room.

As the two Englishmen walked slowly down to the wharf the handsome Captain S—— whistled cheerily, and asked Chester on board to hear him and his steward play violin and piccolo.

"By God, S——," said Chester, "you have no heart!"

"Right you are, my lad. She made it into stone.

But it won't hurt her as it did me. You see, these Frenchmen here pay well for new beauty; and women love money—which is a lucky thing for many men."

THE FEAST AT PENTECOST

The Feast at Pentecost.

THERE was a row in the fo'c's'le of the *Queen Caroline*, barque, of Sydney, and the hands were discussing ways and means upon two subjects—making the skipper give them their usual allowance of rum, or killing him, burning the ship, and clearing out and living among the natives.

Half of the crew were white, the others were Maories, Line Islanders, and Hawaiians. The white men wanted the coloured ones to knock the skipper and two mates on the head, while they slept. The natives declined—but they were quite agreeable to run away on shore with their messmates.

. . . . .

The barque was at anchor at one of the New Hebrides. She was a "sandalwooder," and the captain, Fordham, was, if possible, a greater rascal than any one else on board. He had bargained with the chief of the island for leave to send his crew ashore and cut sandalwood, and on the first day four boat-loads were brought off, whereupon Fordham cursed their laziness. One, an ex-Hobart Town convict, having "talked back," Fordham and the mate tied him up to the pumps and gave him three dozen.

Next day he started the boats away during fierce rain-squalls, and told the men that if they didn't bring plenty of wood he would " haze " them properly.

At dusk they returned and brought word that they had a lot of wood cut, but had left it ashore as the natives would lend them no assistance to load the boats.

The spokesman on this occasion was a big Maori from the Bay of Islands. Fordham gave him three dozen and put him in irons. Then he told the men they would get no supper till the wood was in the barque's hold—and he also stopped their grog.

"Well," said the captain, eyeing them savagely, "what is it going to be? Are you going to get that wood off or not?"

"It's too dark," said one; "and, anyway, we want our supper and grog first."

Fordham made a step towards him, when the whole lot bolted below.

"They'll turn-to early enough to-morrow," said he, grimly, "when they find there's no breakfast for 'em until that wood's on deck." Then he went below to drink rum with his two mates, remarking to his first officer: "You mark my words, Colliss, we're going to have a roasting hot time of it with them fellows here at Pentecost!"

· · · · ·

At daylight next morning the mate, who was less of a brute than the skipper, managed to get some rum and biscuit down into the fo'c's'le; then they turned-to and manned the boats. At noon the second mate, who was in charge of the cutting party, signalled from the shore that something was wrong.

The Feast at Pentecost.

On Fordham reaching the shore the second mate told him that all the native crew had run off into the bush.

The chief of the island was sent for, and Fordham told him to catch the runaways—fourteen in number—promising seven muskets in return. The white crew were working close by in sullen silence. They grinned when they heard the chief say it would be difficult to capture the men; they were natives, he remarked—if they were white men it would be easy enough. But he would try if the captain helped him.

· · · · ·

An hour afterwards the chief was in the bush, talking to the deserters, and taking in an account of the vast amount of trade lying on board the barque.

"See," said he, to the only man among them who spoke his dialect—a Fijian half-caste from Loma-loma—"this is my scheme. The captain of the ship and those that come with him will I entice into the bush and kill them one by one, for the path is narrow——"

"Good," said Sam the half-caste, "and then ten of us, with our hands loosely tied, will be taken off to the ship by two score of your men, who will tell the mate that the captain has caught ten of us, and has gone to seek the other four. Then will the ship be ours."

· · · · ·

"Halloa!" said the mate of the barque to the carpenter, "here's a thundering big crowd of niggers coming off in our two boats, and none of our white chaps with 'em. Stand by, you chaps, with your muskets. I ain't going to let all that crowd aboard with only six men in the ship."

The men left on board watched the progress of the two boats as they were pulled quickly towards the ship. They hardly apprehended any attempt at cutting-off, as from the ship they could discern the figures of some of their shipmates on shore stacking the sandalwood on a ledge of rock, handy for shipping in the boats.

"It's all right," called out the mate presently, "the niggers have collared some of our native chaps. I can see that yaller-hided Fiji Sam sitting aft with his hands lashed behind him. Let 'em come alongside."

. . . . .

"Cap'en been catch him ten men," said the native in charge to the mate, "he go look now find him other fellow four men. He tell me you give me two bottle rum, some tobacco, some biscuit."

"Right you are, you man-catching old cannibal," said the mate, jocosely, "come below." As the mate went below with the native at his heels, the latter made a quick sign by a backward move of his arm. In an instant the ten apparently-bound men had sprung to their feet, and with their pseudo-captors, flung themselves upon the five men. The wild cry of alarm reached the mate in the cabin. He darted up, and as he reached the deck a tomahawk crashed into his brain.

No need to tell the tale of the savage butchery on deck in all its details. Not one of the men had time to even fire a shot—they went down so quickly under the knives and tomahawks of the fifty men who struggled and strove with one another to strike the first blow. One man, indeed, suceeeded in reaching

The Feast at Pentecost.

the main rigging, but ere he had gained ten feet he was stabbed and chopped in half-a-dozen places.

. . . . .

And then, as the remaining members of the crew sat "spelling" in the jungle, and waiting for the skipper's return, there came a sudden, swift rush of dark, naked forms upon them. Then gasping groans and silence.

There were many oven-fires lit that night and the following day; and although the former shipmates of the "long, baked pigs" were present by the invitation of the chief, their uncultivated tastes were satisfied with such simple things as breadfruit and yams.

That was the "wiping-out" of the *Queen Caroline* at Pentecost, and the fulfilment of the unconscious prophecy of Captain Fordham to his mate.

AN HONOUR TO THE SERVICE

An Honour to the Service.

THE Honourable Captain Stanley W—— believed in flogging, and during the three years' cruise of the frigate in the South Pacific he had taken several opportunities of expressing this belief upon the blue-jackets of his ship by practical illustrations of his hobby. He was, however—in his own opinion—a most humane man, and was always ready to give a dozen less if Dr. Cartwright suggested, for instance, that Jenkins or Jones hadn't quite got over his last tricing up, and could hardly stand another dozen so soon. And the chaplain of the frigate, when dining with the Honourable Stanley, would often sigh and shake his head and agree with the captain that the proposed abolition of flogging in the British Navy would do much to destroy its discipline and loosen the feelings of personal attachment between officers and men, and then murmur something complimentary about his Majesty's ship *Pleiades* being one of the very few ships in the Service whose captain still maintained so ancient and honoured a custom, the discontinuance of which could only be advocated by common, illiterate persons—such as the blue-jackets themselves.

. . . . .

The frigate was on her way from Valparaiso to Sydney—it was in the days of Governor Bligh—and for nearly three weeks had been passing amongst the low-lying coral islands of the Paumotu or Low Archipelago, when one afternoon in May, 182– she lay becalmed off the little island of Vairaatea. The sea was as smooth as glass, and only the gentlest ocean swell rose and fell over the flat surface of the coral reef. In those days almost nothing was known of the people of the Paumotu Group except that they were a fierce and warlike race and excessively shy of white strangers. Standing on his quarter-deck Captain W—— could with his glass see that there were but a few houses on the island—perhaps ten—and as the frigate had been nearly six weeks out from Valparaiso, and officers in the navy did not live as luxuriously then as now, he decided to send a boat ashore and buy some turtle from the natives.

"If you can buy a few thousand cocoanuts as well, do so, Mr. T.," said the captain, "and I'll send another boat later on."

·   ·   ·   ·   ·

The boat's crew was well armed, and in command of the second lieutenant. Among them was a man named Hallam, a boatswain's mate, a dark-faced, surly brute of about fifty. He was hated by nearly every one on board, but as he was a splendid seaman and rigidly exact in the performance of his duties, he was an especial favourite of the captain's, who was never tired of extolling his abilities and sobriety, and holding him up as an example of a British seaman: and Hallam, like his captain, was a firm believer in the cat.

·   ·   ·   ·   ·

On pulling in to the beach about a dozen light-skinned natives met them. They were all armed with clubs and spears, but at a sign from one who seemed to be their chief they laid them down All—the chief as well—were naked, save for a girdle of long grass round their loins.

Their leader advanced to Lieutenant T—— as he stepped out of the boat, and holding out his hand said, "Good mornin'. What you want?"

Pleased at finding a man who spoke English, the lieutenant told him he had come to buy some turtle and get a boatload of young cocoanuts, and showed him the tobacco and knives intended for payment.

The chief's eyes glistened at the tobacco; the others, who did not know its use, turned away in indifference, but eagerly handled the knives.

· · · · ·

All this time the chief's eyes kept wandering to the face of Hallam, the boatswain's mate, whose every movement he followed with a curious, wistful expression. Suddenly he turned to the lieutenant and said, in curious broken English, that cocoanuts were easily to be obtained, but turtle were more difficult; yet if the ship would wait he would promise to get them as many as were wanted by daylight next morning.

"All right," said Lieutenant T——, "bear a hand with the cocoanuts now, and I'll tell the captain what you say"; and then to Hallam, "If this calm keeps up, Hallam, I'm afraid the ship will either have to anchor or tow off the land—she's drifting in fast."

In an hour the boat was filled with cocoanuts, and Lieutenant T—— sent her off to the ship with a note to the captain, remaining himself with Hallam, another leading seaman named Lacy, and five bluejackets. Presently the chief, in his strange, halting English, asked the officer to come to his house and sit down and rest while his wife prepared food for him. And as they walked the native's eyes still sought the face of Hallam the boatswain.

His wife was a slender, graceful girl, and her modest, gentle demeanour as she waited upon her husband himself impressed the lieutenant considerably.

"Where did you learn to speak English?" the officer asked his host after they had finished.

He answered slowly, "I been sailor man American whaleship two year;" and then, pointing to a roll of soft mats, said, "You like sleep, you sleep. Me like go talk your sailor man."

. . . . .

Hallam, morose and gloomy, had left the others, and was sitting under the shade of a *toa*-tree, when he heard the sound of a footstep, and looking up saw the dark-brown, muscular figure of the native chief beside him.

"Well," he said, surlily, "what the h—— do you want?"

The man made him no answer—only looked at him with a strange, eager light of expectancy in his eyes, and his lips twitched nervously, but no sound issued from them. For a moment the rude, scowling face of the old seaman seemed to daunt him. Then, with a curious choking sound in his throat, he sprang forward and touched the other man on the arm.

"*Father!* Don't you know me?"

With trembling hands and blanched face the old

man rose to his feet, and in a hoarse whisper there escaped from his lips a name that he had long years ago cursed and forgotten. His hands opened and shut again convulsively, and then his savage, vindictive nature asserted itself again as he found his voice, and with the rasping accents of passion poured out curses, upon the brown, half-naked man that stood before him. Then he turned to go. But the other man put out a detaining hand.

. . . . .

"It is as you say. I am a disgraced man. But you haven't heard why I deserted from the *Tagus*. Listen while I tell you. I was flogged. I was only a boy, and it broke my heart."

"Curse you, you chicken-hearted sweep! I've laid the cat on the back of many a better man than myself, and none of 'em ever disgraced themselves by runnin' away and turnin' into a nigger, like you!"

The man heard the sneer with unmoved face, then resumed—

"It broke my heart. And when I was hiding in Dover, and my mother used to come and dress my wounds, do you remember what happened?"

"Aye, you naked swab, I do: your father kicked you out!"

"And I got caught again, and put in irons, and got more cat. Two years afterwards I cleared again in Sydney, from the *Sirius*. . . . And I came here to live and die among savages. That's nigh on eight years ago."

. . . . .

There was a brief silence. The old man, with

fierce, scornful eyes, looked sneeringly at the wild figure of the broken wanderer, and then said—

"What's to stop me from telling our lieutenant you're a deserter? I would, too, by God, only I don't want my shipmates to know I've got a nigger for a son."

The gibe passed unheeded, save for a sudden light that leapt into the eyes of the younger man, then quickly died away.

"Let us part in peace," he said. "We will never meet again. Only tell me one thing—is my mother dead?"

"Yes."

"Thank God for that," he murmured. Then without another word the outcast turned away and disappeared among the cocoa-palms.

. . . . .

The second boat from the *Pleiades* brought the captain, and as he and the lieutenant stood and talked they watched the natives carrying down the cocoa-nuts.

"Hurry them up, Hallam," said Lieutenant T——; "the tide is falling fast. By the by, where is that fellow Lacy; I don't see him about?"

As he spoke a woman's shriek came from the chief's house, which stood some distance apart from the other houses, and a tall brown man sprang out from among the other natives about the boats and dashed up the pathway to the village.

"Quick, Hallam, and some of you fellows," said Captain W——, "run and see what's the matter. That scoundrel, Lacy, I suppose, among the women," he added, with a laugh, to the lieutenant.

. . . . .

An Honour to the Service. 289

The two officers followed the men. In a few minutes they came upon a curious scene. Held in the strong arms of two stout seamen was the native chief, whose heaving chest and working features showed him to be under some violent emotion. On the ground, with his head supported by a shipmate, lay Lacy, with blackened and distorted face, and breathing stertorously. Shaking with fear and weeping passionately as she pressed her child to her bosom, the young native wife looked beseechingly into the faces of the men who held her husband.

"What is the meaning of this?" said Captain W——'s clear, sharp voice, addressing the men who held the chief.

"That hound there"—the men who held their prisoner nearly let him go in their astonishment—"came in here. She was alone. Do you want to know more? I tried to kill him."

"Let him loose, men," and Captain W—— stepped up to the prisoner and looked closely into his dark face. "Ah! I thought so—a white man. What is your name?"

The wanderer bent his head, then raised it, and looked for an instant at the sullen face of Hallam.

. . . . .

"I have no name," he said.

"Humph," muttered Captain W—— to his lieutenant, "a runaway convict, most likely. He can't be blamed, though, for this affair. He's a perfect brute, that fellow Lacy." Then to the strange white man he turned contemptuously:

"I'm sorry this man assaulted your wife. He shall suffer for it to-morrow. At the same time I'm sorry

I can't tie *you* up and flog you, as a disgrace to your colour and country, you naked savage."

The outcast took two strides, a red gleam shone in his eyes, and his voice shook with mad passion.

"'A naked savage'; and you would like to flog me. It was a brute such as you made me what I am," and he struck the captain of the *Pleiades* in the face with his clenched hand.

. . . . .

"We'll have to punish the fellow, T——," said Captain W——, as with his handkerchief to his lips he staunched the flow of blood. "If I let a thing like this pass his native friends would imagine all sorts of things and probably murder any unfortunate merchant captain that may touch here in the future. But, as Heaven is my witness, I do so on that ground only—deserter as he admits himself to be. Hurry up that fellow, T——."

. . . . .

"That fellow" was Hallam, who had been sent to the boat for a bit of line suitable for the purpose in view. His florid face paled somewhat when the coxswain jeeringly asked him if he didn't miss his green bag, and flung him an old pair of yoke-lines.

. . . . .

The business of flogging was not, on the whole, unduly hurried. Although "All Hands to Witness Punishment" was not piped, every native on the island, some seventy or so all told, gathered round the cocoanut-tree to which the man was lashed, and at every stroke of the heavy yoke-lines they shuddered. One, a woman with a child sitting beside her, lay face to the ground, and as each cruel swish and thud fell on her ear the savage creature wept.

.   .   .   .   .

"That's enough, Hallam," said Captain W——, somewhat moved by the tears and bursting sobs of the pitying natives, who, when they saw the great blue weals on the brown back swell and black drops burst out, sought to break in through the cordon of blue jackets.

.   .   .   .   .

Clustering around him, the brown people sought to lift him in their arms and carry him to his house; but his strength was not all gone, and he thrust them aside. Then he spoke, and even the cold, passionless Captain W—— felt his face flush at the burning words:

"For seven years, lads, I've lived here, a naked savage, as your captain called me. I had a heavy disgrace once, an' it just broke my heart like—I was flogged—and I wanted to hide myself out of the world. Seven years it is since I saw a white man, an' I've almost forgotten I *was* a white man once; an' now because I tried to choke a hound that wanted to injure the only being in the world I have to love, I'm tied up and lashed like a dog—*by my own father!*

.   .   .   .   .

The island was just sinking below the horizon when the burly figure of boatswain's mate Hallam was seen to disappear suddenly over the bows, where he had been standing.

.   .   .   .   .

"A very regrettable occurrence," said Captain W——, pompously, to the chaplain when the boats returned from the search. "No doubt the horror of seeing his only son a disgraced fugitive and severed from all decent associations preyed upon his mind and led him to commit suicide. Such men as Hallam, humble as was his position, are an Honour to the Service. I shall always remember him as a very zealous seaman."

"Particularly with the cat," murmured Lieutenant T——.

J. B. LIPPINCOTT COMPANY'S
PUBLICATIONS BY
POPULAR AUTHORS.

BY
ANNE HOLLINGSWORTH WHARTON.

Through Colonial Doorways.

With a number of colonial illustrations from drawings specially made for the work. 12mo. Cloth, $1.25.

"It is a pleasant retrospect of fashionable New York and Philadelphia society during and immediately following the Revolution; for there was a Four Hundred even in those days, and some of them were Whigs and some were Tories, but all enjoyed feasting and dancing, of which there seemed to be no limit. And this little book tells us about the belles of the Philadelphia meschianza, who they were, how they dressed, and how they flirted with Major André and other officers in Sir William Howe's wicked employ."—*Philadelphia Record*.

Colonial Days and Dames.

With numerous illustrations. 12mo. Cloth, $1.25.

"In less skilful hands than those of Anne Hollingsworth Wharton's, these scraps of reminiscences from diaries and letters would prove but dry bones. But she has made them so charming that it is as if she had taken dried roses from an old album and freshened them into bloom and perfume. Each slight paragraph from a letter is framed in historical sketches of local affairs or with some account of the people who knew the letter writers, or were at least of their date, and there are pretty suggestions as to how and why such letters were written, with hints of love affairs, which lend a rose-colored veil to what were probably every-day matters in colonial families."—*Pittsburg Bulletin*.

For sale by all Booksellers, or will be sent, post-paid, upon receipt of price,

J. B. LIPPINCOTT COMPANY, Publishers,
PHILADELPHIA.

MISS CAREY'S STORIES FOR GIRLS.

LITTLE MISS MUFFET.
COUSIN MONA.

12mo. Cloth, illustrated, $1.25 per volume.

The two above volumes, in box, $2.50.

With great descriptive power, considerable and often quiet fun, there is a delicacy and tenderness, a knowledge and strength of purpose, combined with so much fertility of resource and originality that the interest never flags, and the sensation on putting down any of her works is that of having dwelt in a thoroughly healthy atmosphere.

MERLE'S CRUSADE.
AUNT DIANA.   ESTHER.
OUR BESSIE.   AVERIL.

12mo. Cloth, $1.25 per volume.

Five volumes, uniform binding, in neat box, $6.25.

"Miss Rosa Nouchette Carey has achieved an enviable reputation as a writer of tales of a restful and quiet kind. They tell pleasant stories of agreeable people, are never sensational, and have a genuine moral purpose and helpful tone, without being aggressively didactic or distinctly religious in character."—*N. Y. Christian Union.*

For sale by all Booksellers, or will be sent, post-paid, upon receipt of price,

J. B. LIPPINCOTT COMPANY, Publishers,
PHILADELPHIA.

MRS. A. L. WISTER.

Translations from the German.

$1.00 per volume.

Countess Erika's Apprenticeship. By Ossip Schubin.
"O Thou, My Austria!" By Ossip Schubin.
Erlach Court. By Ossip Schubin.
The Alpine Fay. By E. Werner.
  The Owl's Nest. By E. Marlitt.
  Picked Up in the Streets. By H. Schobert.
  Saint Michael. By E. Werner.
  Violetta. By Ursula Zoge von Manteufel.
The Lady with the Rubies. By E. Marlitt.
Vain Forebodings. By E. Oswald.
A Penniless Girl. By W. Heimburg.
Quicksands. By Adolph Streckfuss.
  Countess Gisela. By E. Marlitt.
  At the Councillor's. By E. Marlitt.
  The Second Wife. By E. Marlitt.
  The Old Mam'selle's Secret. By E. Marlitt.
Gold Elsie. By E. Marlitt.
The Little Moorland Princess. By E. Marlitt.
Banned and Blessed. By E. Werner.
A Noble Name. By Claire von Glümer.

MRS. WISTER'S TRANSLATIONS.
Continued.

From Hand to Hand. By Golo Raimund.

Severa. By E. Hartner.

A New Race. By Golo Raimund.

The Eichhofs. By Moritz von Reichenbach.

Castle Hohenwald. By Adolph Streckfuss.

Margarethe. By E. Juncker.

Too Rich. By Adolph Streckfuss.

A Family Feud. By Ludwig Harder.

The Green Gate. By Ernst Wichert.

Only a Girl. By Wilhelmine von Hillern.

Why Did He Not Die. By Ad. von Volckhauser.

Hulda. By Fanny Lewald.

The Bailiff's Maid. By E. Marlitt.

In the Schillingscourt. By E. Marlitt.

"Mrs. A. L. Wister, through her many translations of novels from the German, has established a reputation of the highest order for literary judgment, and for a long time her name upon the title-page of such a translation has been a sufficient guarantee to the lovers of fiction of a pure and elevating character, that the novel would be a cherished home favorite. This faith in Mrs. Wister is fully justified by the fact that among her more than thirty translations that have been published by Lippincott's there has not been a single disappointment. And to the exquisite judgment of selection is to be added the rare excellence of her translations, which has commanded the admiration of literary and linguistic scholars."
—*Boston Home Journal.*

J. B. Lippincott Company, Philadelphia.

Authors and Their Works.

"THE DUCHESS."

Lady Patty.   Peter's Wife.   A Little Irish Girl.
The Hoyden.

12mo. Paper, 50 cents; cloth, $1.00.

Phyllis.	Mrs. Geoffrey.
Molly Bawn.	Portia.
Airy Fairy Lilian.	Löys, Lord Berresford, and
Beauty's Daughters.	other Stories.
Faith and Unfaith.	Rossmoyne.
Doris.	A Mental Struggle.
"O Tender Dolores."	Lady Valworth's Diamonds.
A Maiden All Forlorn.	Lady Branksmere.
In Durance Vile.	A Modern Circe.
The Duchess.	The Honourable Mrs. Vere-
Marvel.	ker.
Jerry, and other Stories.	Under-Currents.

A Life's Remorse.

Bound only in Cloth, $1.00.

"'The Duchess' has well deserved the title of being one of the most fascinating novelists of the day. The stories written by her are the airiest, lightest, and brightest imaginable; full of wit, spirit, and gayety, yet containing touches of the most exquisite pathos. There is something good in all of them."—*London Academy.*

J. B. Lippincott Company, Philadelphia.

Authors and Their Works.

Mrs. H. Lovett Cameron.

A Tragic Blunder.
A Daughter's Heart. A Sister's Sin.
Jack's Secret.

12mo. Paper, 50 cents; cloth, $1.00.

"Mrs. Cameron's novels, 'In a Grass Country,' 'A Daughter's Heart,' 'A Sister's Sin,' 'Jack's Secret,' have shown a high skill in inventing interesting plots and delineating character. All her stories are vivid in action and pure in tone. This one, 'A Tragic Blunder,' is equal to her best."—*National Tribune.*

This Wicked World.
In a Grass Country.   A Devout Lover.
Vera Neville.   A Life's Mistake.
Pure Gold.   Worth Winning.
The Cost of a Lie.   A Lost Wife.

Cloth, $1.00.

"The works of this author are always pure in character, and can be safely put into the hands of young as well as old."—*Norristown Herald.*

"A wide circle of admirers always welcome a new work by this favorite author. Her style is pure and interesting, and she depicts marvellously well the daily social life of the English people."—*St. Louis Republic.*

J. B. Lippincott Company, Philadelphia.

Authors and Their Works.

JULIEN GORDON.

"Now and then, to prove to men—perhaps also to prove to themselves—what they can do if they dare and will, one of these gifted women detaches herself from her sisters, enters the arena with men, to fight for the highest prizes, and as the brave Gotz says of Brother Martin, 'shames many a knight.' To this race of conquerors belongs to-day one of the first living writers of novels and romances, Julien Gordon."

FRIEDRICH SPIELHAGEN.

Poppæa.
A Diplomat's Diary.
A Successful Man.
Vampires, and Mademoiselle Réséda.
Two stories in one book.

12mo. Cloth, $1.00 per vol.

"The cleverness and lightness of touch which characterized 'A Diplomat's Diary' are not wanting in the later work of the American lady who writes under the pseudonyme of Julien Gordon. In her former story the dialogue is pointed and alert, the characters are clear-cut and distinct, and the descriptions picturesque. As for the main idea of 'A Successful Man,' the intersection of two wholly different strata of American life,—one fast and fashionable, the other domestic and decorous,—it is worked out with much skill and alertness of treatment to its inevitably tragic issue."—*N. Y. World.*

J. B. Lippincott Company, Philadelphia.

www.ingramcontent.com/pod-product-compliance
Lightning Source LLC
Chambersburg PA
CBHW030817230426
43667CB00008B/1256